Dynamic Dimensional Designs

Contents

Foreword

Innovative, creative, fresh and fun is how I describe Sallie J. Russell's new book, **Dynamic Dimensional Designs.**

Through the years I've watched Sallie try, test, perfect and teach some of the inspiring techniques she shares in this book. I admire her unusual ability to take a simple idea, like decorative stitching, and give it a new twist by using it as a foundation for "Stitch 'N Weave," which opens up endless possibilities for the wearable artist. What a great way to combine wonderful yarns and cords into a stitched piece.

Sallie's Puff-liqué literally takes appliqué to new heights and her ideas are adaptable to garments or home decorating. The dimension makes any design come to life!

Throughout the text, Sallie offers options in materials and methods, so there's something for everyone's taste and skill level.

This book, with its clearly written instructions and accompanying illustrations, can open up new horizons even for those who've not ventured in the world of embellishment before.

I hope you find this book as inspiring as I have and use it to guide your own creative endeavors.

Pauline Richards
Publisher, Total Embellishment Newsletter

Chapter 1

Stitch 'N Weave

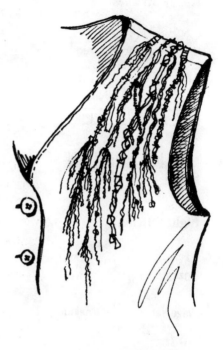

Shoulder Scroll Accent
Chapter 9

Stitch 'N Weave is a technique where decorative yarns, threads, cords or ribbons are woven through pre-sewn machine stitching . . . twisting, turning, looping or knotting if desired. The machine stitched patterns can be abstract, specific design shapes or used for borders. These patterns of multiple-stitched rows can also be a tone-on-tone design element without the weaving. Add the thread weaving at a later time and your friends and colleagues will think it's a new garment! Unlike couching, the yarns can be exchanged for new colors and textures next season by gently pulling out the original yarns and weaving in new ones. Use this embellishing technique on both ready-to-wear and made-to-wear garments!

Projects using the Stitch 'N Weave technique are found in Chapter 9 - Stitch 'N Weave Designs and Chapter 13 - Harvest Time.

Stitching Choices

Suitable machine stitches for this technique have a wide stitch width (3mm or wider) without an intermediate stitch, as they swing across the stitch width. To showcase the weaving, stitch with machine embroidery thread that matches or blends with the fabric background. To add a bit of sparkle, stitch with metallic thread.

SJR Tip A detachable vest or jacket lapel is a great place to experiment with this technique or incorporate it into a multi-media design on a shirt shawl (see projects in Chapters 9 and 13).

Heavy Stitches

VVVVVVVV
Rickrack or Triple Zigzag

| | | | | | | | | | |
Blanket

⊓⊔⊓⊔⊓⊔⊓⊔
Ladder

\▧▧\▧▧\▧▧\▧▧\▧
Satin Block

Light Stitches

∨∨∨∨∨∨∨∨
Zigzag

‾_‾_‾_‾_‾
Universal or Elastic Casing

___∧___∧__∧
Blind Hem

∨∨∨∨∨∨∨∨∨∨
Overlock

SJR Tip A great place to find exciting yarns, cords and ribbons is in your local knitting, needlework, or weaving store. They have wonderful textured and sparkly yarns on cards or small packages and in larger skeins.

Heavy stitches like the rickrack or triple zigzag, blanket, ladder and satin block stitches will be more visible than those with less stitch repetition. Light stitches include the standard zigzag, universal or elastic casing stitch, blind hem and some overlock or overedge stitches.

It's always a good idea to test, checking the stitch pattern with the particular weaving materials you plan to use. For example, when using a narrow or single yarn use a narrower stitch width. Narrower stitches (3mm) may have to be lengthened slightly to give enough "display room" for fuzzy or wispy yarns. Zigzag stitches are good for heavier or stiffer weaving materials, while the ladder or blanket stitches better secure the lighter, wispy yarns.

Weaving Materials

Use any decorative yarns, threads, cords or ribbons that can be woven under the machine's crosswise stitches. If they can be threaded through a double-eye needle they probably can be used to weave. With some stitch patterns that create long lengthwise stitches, like the ladder or blanket stitch, you can choose to weave in both directions. Yarns with metallic threads are rough and tend to catch on the stitched threads. These and heavy, slubby yarns do not have to be woven under every cross stitch, instead weave them over and under evenly or randomly spaced stitches. Use cords or heavy decorative threads for a "punch" of color along with the yarns.

There are several companies that package 5 to 10 yard assortments of yarns in a particular color grouping (see Sources, page 70). These cards have plenty of yarn for an average project. If the yarns are slim, twist and weave two together; add ribbon or other cords to the blend for texture or to give a color punch.

Weaving with ribbons can create a different texture. Satin or grosgrain ribbons need to be narrower than the stitch width, because of their bulk. However, soft and supple silk ribbons can be wider than the stitch width. Knotting or twisting the ribbons adds additional texture to a Stitch 'N Weave project.

Weaving Notions

Use a double-eye needle for the weaving process. The flat, blunt end makes the needle easy to feed under the stitches, especially those with repeating stitch patterns. Any yarns, ribbons or cords that can be threaded through a double-eye needle can be used for Stitch 'N Weave. A tapestry needle can be used, but more care will need to be taken to prevent the point from splitting the repeating stitch patterns.

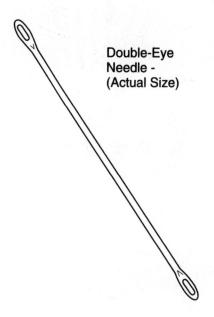

Double-Eye Needle - (Actual Size)

Other notions include:
- Water or air soluble marking pen to mark the basic design stitching lines on the fabric, a permanent marking pen to draw on water soluble stabilizer
- Seam sealant to keep the cut ends of the thread or yarn from fraying
- Tear-away stabilizer to place under the design area when stitching

Stitch 'N Weave Basics

Always check your stitch and yarn combination for compatibility, before starting the actual project. "Test drive" using your weaving materials with various stitches on your project fabric.

Stitching:

Draw the design lines on the fabric right side with the marking pen, or draw the design onto a water soluble stabilizer using a permanent marking pen and pin it to the right side of the fabric. Place-tear away stabilizer underneath the design area.

Stitch with machine embroidery thread in the needle and all-purpose or bobbin thread in the bobbin. If the project's underside will not be concealed by a facing, use matching thread in the bobbin for a neater look.

SJR Tip A needle or floss threader will aid in threading the bulkier and wispy yarns through the needle eye.

Cut ribbon ends on the diagonal for easier threading.

3

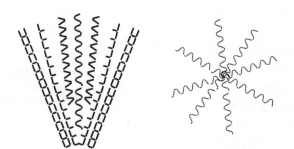

Stitching lines should not cross, but dovetail for a tighter design pattern. However, the stitching for designs that radiate out from a center can cross. For solid design areas allow 1/4" between the stitching rows.

After stitching, secure the thread ends. This can be done by hand tying a knot in the threads; lowering the feed dogs and stitching in place several stitches; or using the fix or stop feature on your machine.

Remove water soluble stabilizer before weaving. The tear-away stabilizer can be removed before or after the weaving is completed.

Weaving:

Thread one end of the double-eye needle with yarn and weave the unthreaded end over and under the long stitches. Use one or more yarns — whatever will feed under the threads. Cords or heavy decorative thread can be twisted with the yarns or woven separately in their own pattern.

Work with strands approximately 18" in length or shorter and keep one end of the single strand close to the threaded needle eye. To secure the strands when beginning to weave, loop the ends over one or more of the machine stitches, similar to a backstitch. Weave short spans, pulling the strand through looping or knotting as desired.

Short Tail

The following weaving techniques indicate certain types of yarn. Actual projects using these yarns are listed in parentheses. Other yarn types can be used – remember test combinations.

SJR Tip Playing with the yarn on a sample or even on THE project lets you see just how you'll have to manipulate that particular yarn. Keep the yarn slack in the weaving process, even to the point of being loopy, but anchor it frequently with the backstitch. Too tightly pulled strands will not fill in the design easily or quickly. Remember this is not a technique for frequently washed items! However, the yarns can be removed to change the color palate or to replace worn looking pieces.

Yarns with long "eyelashes" need to have the "lashes" pulled loose while weaving. Use the blunt end of the needle to pull loops in the woven yarn to loosen the wispy threads. Anchor these yarns frequently with a backstitch over one stitch. (Chapters 9 - Stitch 'N Weave and 13 - Harvest Time)

Chenille yarns look great with tiny loops pulled between the cross stitches, pinch the loop and twist; or create loops by backstitching over two stitches. The post vine on the front cover uses this technique. (Chapters 9 and 13)

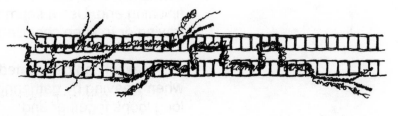

Twisted   Backstitched

Use short pieces of yarn with the same length tails and weave them between two stitched rows, cutting the yarns to remove the needle. This is effective as a border, stripe, or as a trim on a garment edge as illustrated on the next page.

Cut yarns with random large nubs on either side of the protrusion. To place the nubs, weave from each yarn end separately placing the nub over several stitches. (See Chapter 9, Photo 13 and Back Cover)

Tie knots in satin or grosgrain ribbons at intervals as they are woven or twist the ribbon by passing over several stitches then weave it under again for more texture. (See Chapter 9 and Photo 8)

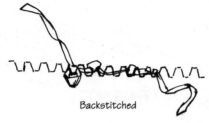

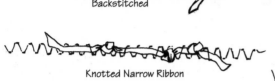

Backstitched

Use a backstitch with narrow silk ribbon for a smooth raised look (Chapter 9, Photo 13 and Back Cover) or knots to give a bumpy texture. Knots tied loosely in wider silk ribbons create a stunning effect and make a wonderful border application.

Knotted Narrow Ribbon

Knotted Wide Ribbon

The finishing ends of the yarns can be woven into the design and hidden or they can be left free for a fringe effect. Backstitch near the end of the weaving to secure the finishing end. Use a seam sealant to prevent the ends from fraying or to keep chenille-like yarns from losing their fluff.

A tassel can be created when weaving by gathering long loops together and wrapping with a piece of yarn. Start weaving away from where the tassel will form; leave a long loop before continuing the weaving in the opposite direction.

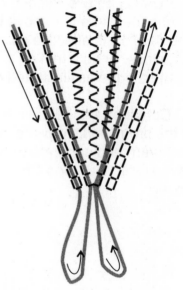

To form a tassel, wrap and tie two or three 4" long yarn pieces tightly around the hanging loops; secure the yarn ends under the design edge. (See Chapter 9, Page 43, Shield and Tassel Lapel)

Stitch 'N Weave Edge Trim

Chapter 2

Puff-liqué

The Puff-liqué technique adapts appliqué shapes or print fabric designs and uses a water soluble stabilizer to turn under the edges of the design. Fiberfill is inserted into the pouch formed between the fabric and the stabilizer. The design is then stitched to the base fabric with either a straight, blind hem or zigzag stitch. Further dimension is created by stitching on interior design lines. A variation of Puff-liqué uses fleece layers instead of fiberfill, allowing more control over the dimension.

The Pumpkin Design Above Is The Reverse Of The Patterns In Chapter 13

Some designs need to be simplified when used for Puff-liqué. The maple leaf will be as effective with some of the points removed, making it easier to adapt to this technique.

Projects that use the Puff-liqué and its variations are Chapters 8 - Spring Garden, 9 - Stitch 'N Weave Designs, 10 - Flower Basket and 13 - Harvest Time.

Puff-liqué Materials

The following materials are needed for the Puff-liqué technique:

- Fusible stabilizer for tracing patterns
- Water soluble stabilizer (regular weight) for help in turning edges under and holding fiberfill
- Fiberfill or fusible fleece to puff the designs
- Water soluble or other removable marking pen
- Wonder Tape, a water soluble, double-sided sew through basting tape or pins to hold designs in place
- Machine embroidery thread for detail stitching
- Monofilament thread for invisible stitching

> **SJR Tip**
> The designs in this book are mirror images of the finished designs. Remember that letters and numbers have to be traced in reverse to be read on the finished design. Other designs like leaves can be traced in reverse for more variety.

Puff-liqué Basics

Trace the Puff-liqué design onto the matte side of a fusible stabilizer, like Sulky's Totally Stable. Cut out the traced design and fuse it to the fabric wrong side.

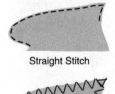

To the fabric right side, pin a piece of water soluble stabilizer. Straight stitch around the outer edges of the design using a short (2mm) stitch length. Trim the fabric and water soluble stabilizer, leaving a scant 1/4" outside the stitching line. Clip to the stitching line on the inside corners or curves and trim off the outside corners. Remove the fusible stabilizer pattern.

Cut a 1" slit in the water soluble stabilizer only and turn the design right side out through the opening, using serger tweezers as needed. (Tweezer points make it easier to go in, pinch the design corner and pull it out.) Use a wooden point turner to help push out all the design contours. Press with a <u>dry</u> iron on the fabric side.

Carefully separate the stabilizer from the fabric and use tweezers to insert small amounts of fiberfill through the opening. The fiberfill should be distributed evenly over the design but not tightly packed.

Straight Stitch

Zigzag

Blindhem

When combining Puff-liqué with traditional appliqué, apply design elements from the base fabric out. Those closer to the surface, including the Puff-liqué may overlap flat portions of the design. Pin the Puff-liqué in place on the base fabric and stitch around the edges. Because the fabric raw edges are folded under, you can stitch with a straight stitch, a blind hem stitch or a narrow zigzag (1-1.5mm length and width).

8

When stitching Puff-liqué interior design lines and outer edges, lighten your machine pressure, if possible. On the interior design lines, straight stitch (3mm length) with machine embroidery thread. This stitching will give the design more dimension and hold the fiberfill in place.

Dissolve the water soluble stabilizer by spraying the area with water or dipping the design in warm water.

SJR Tip To remove large amounts of water soluble stabilizer, soak the item in warm water for a few minutes, then rinse. Roll in a towel to remove excess water and hang to dry.

Puff-liqué With Printed Fabrics

Printed fabrics can be a wonderful source for quick Puff-liqué designs. The Fireworks flag and firecracker designs in Chapter 9 and Photo 5 are made from printed fabrics. (The balloon shirt (Photo 7) is also made from printed fabric.) Designs should be at least 1 1/2", as smaller designs are hard to manipulate. When it is not possible to Puff-liqué the entire design, use a more traditional method for the smaller portions. Mix your embellishment media and combine Puff-liqué with more traditional appliqué and use machine stitching for details.

Since the pattern is already printed on the fabric, place the water soluble stabilizer on the right side of the fabric design and stitch, trim, clip and turn according to the Puff-liqué basic instructions.

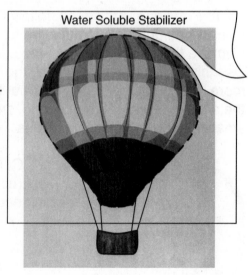

Water Soluble Stabilizer

Insert the fiberfill and position the design on the base fabric. Stitch around the outer design edges using a straight, a blind hem or a small zigzag stitch.

Apply smaller sections, like the balloon basket, using traditional appliqué methods.

Use machine embroidery thread to enhance the design. Straight stitch along some of the design lines, like the contour lines on the balloon, to give added dimension and hold the fiberfill in place. Replace the design lines, like those that were cut away between the basket and balloon, with one or more rows of straight or free-motion machine stitching. Dissolve the stabilizer as noted previously.

Puff-liqué With Fleece

To give large objects (2" or more), like a pumpkin or basket, more dimension, substitute fleece layers for the fiberfill. Not all sections need to be puffed and some sections may have more layers than others. On garments be careful the design area doesn't get too stiff from the amount or number of fleece layers used. (See Chapters 8 - Spring Garden, 10 - Flower Basket and 13 - Harvest Time for projects)

To Puff-liqué with fleece, follow the basic Puff-liqué instructions until you remove the fusible stabilizer pattern. Remove the pattern inside of the stitching lines carefully. Use this as a pattern for cutting the fleece layer(s). When more than one layer is needed, cut the larger layer first, then the smaller layer; cut the second, smaller layer slightly smaller along the common edges.

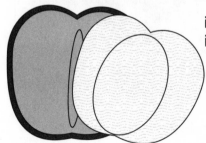

Continue with the basic instructions, inserting fleece instead of the fiberfill.

SJR Tip

Use fusible fleece cut with the pattern right side up on the fleece fusing side. Insert the layers into the pouch and fuse the fleece to the design fabric's wrong side by pressing on the fabric side with a <u>dry</u> iron.

To attach the fleece Puff-liqué to the base fabric, pin or Wonder Tape it in place and mark on the fabric right side, along the interior design lines (fleece edges). Straight stitch (3-4mm length) along these lines first, with a dark color machine embroidery thread to emphasize the dimension. After stitching the interior design lines, stitch the edges down following the Puff-liqué basic directions.

Ultrasuede or Craft Felt Variation

Using faux suede or felt is a quick way to Puff-liqué because the no-fray edges do not require finishing.

Trace the design onto the matte side of a fusible stabilizer and fuse it to the fabric wrong side. Cut out the design along the traced edges.

Remove the fusible stabilizer pattern and use the interior portion to cut the fleece layer(s). Cut the fleece pieces slightly smaller along the outer design edges. Place the fleece layer(s) on the fabric wrong side.

Pin the design in place on the base. Mark the interior lines (fleece edges). Stitch to highlight the designs dimensions, using either a dark machine embroidery thread and a straight stitch or an invisible thread and a small zigzag.

Use monofilament thread to stitch the design edges to the base with a small zigzag.

SJR Tip To cut fusible fleece, pin the pattern right side up on the fusing side of the fleece. Fuse the larger fleece piece to the appliqué wrong side and the smaller piece in place on the larger.

Dimensional Design Ideas

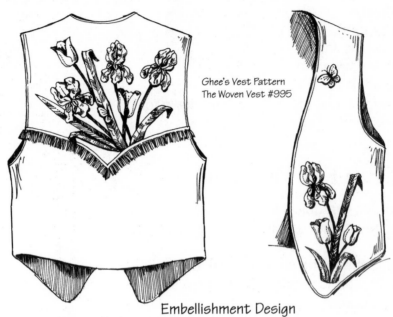

Ghee's Vest Pattern
The Woven Vest #995

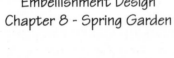

Embellishment Design
Chapter 8 - Spring Garden

Vest Embellishment
Chapter 7 - Cardinal's Roost

Flowered Lapel
Chapter 5 - Detachable Lapels
Chapter 10 - Flower Basket

Chapter 3

Dimensional Appliqué

Spring Garden
Shirt Shawl Front
Chapter 8

This technique involves stitching Ultra-suede or other faux suede designs dimensionally by allowing the edges to remain loose and/or creating *bubbles* in the partially stitched pieces. Stitching tucks or darts within the design also creates dimension. Use any of these dimensional appliqué stitching methods for a quick and painless way to add depth to your basic design. Then the fun comes enhancing the basic design with decorative threads or ribbons, in the form of branches, spiral curly-q's etc.

Craft felt can also be used for dimensional appliqué designs using stitching methods one and two described later in this chapter. Using the other stitching methods requires no-fray fabric with more draping characteristics and stretch than craft felt.

Dimensional Appliqué Materials

The following materials are needed for the dimensional appliqué techniques:
- Ultrasuede, craft felt or any other non-fraying material
- Monofilament thread for an invisible application
- Rayon or metallic machine embroidery thread for detailing
- Tear-away stabilizer placed under the base fabric
- Fusible stabilizer, like Sulky's Totally Stable, for a reusable design template
- Wonder Tape, a water soluble, double-sided sew-through basting tape to hold the designs in place

Dimensional Appliqué Basics

Trace the design onto the matte side of a fusible stabilizer, rough cut the design and fuse to the fabric wrong side. To emphasize the dimensional appearance, place the designs with their interior stitching lines going <u>with</u> the fabric stretch allowing the suede to be stretched slightly as it is stitched. Cut out the design and remove the stabilizer pattern. The designs in this book are mirror images of the finished designs. Remember that letters and numbers must be traced in reverse to be read on the finished design. Other designs like the leaves can be traced in reverse for more variety. For additional variety reduce or enlarge the designs with a copy machine.

Mark any placement lines and place a tear-away stabilizer under the design area on the fabric wrong side. Apply any underlying designs or other embellishments like Stitch 'N Weave, couching, etc. to the base before the dimensional appliqué.

Dimensional Stitching Techniques

Arrange the design pieces on the base fabric, remove the overlapping pieces and pin or Wonder Tape the remaining pieces in place. Stitch the design to the base following one of these stitching methods.

Method One

Stitch the center design lines with a 3mm straight stitch and use contrasting machine embroidery thread for design emphasis. Insert a pencil or dowel between design lines to give the design more dimension (bubble) after it is stitched.

This is an easy method for a beginning embellishment project. It's great for appliquéing leaves in Chapters 12 - Cascading Leaves, 13 - Harvest time and 14 - Poinsettia and Holly.

Method Two

Edgestitch one edge of the design down, leaving the opposite side or portions of the design unstitched. Stitch with monofilament thread in the needle and matching bobbin thread. Use a small zigzag (1 or 1.5mm stitch width and length) or a 2.5mm straight stitch. Use this method for applying the cardinal in Chapter 7 - Cardinal's Roost and for attaching flower stems in Chapter 8 - Spring Garden.

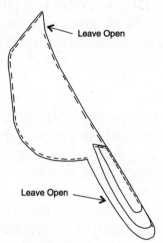

Leave Open

Leave Open

SJR Tip For invisible edgestitching on napped material, rough up the nap along the stitched line with a soft brush or your finger nail to make the stitches disappear.

Method Three

To simulate multiple parts and their dimension on small and some large designs, cut them out in one piece and build the dimension in by stitching tucks or darts. Fold the Ultrasuede design right sides together; place a piece of stabilizer under the folded design; stitch a tuck or dart close to the fold. When stitching double-end curved darts, stop in the middle with needle in fabric, raise the presser foot and rearrange the fabric with the curve of the dart. The darts do not have to be stitched as precisely as garment darts, the difference in each one will give every flower its unique shape. Remove the designs from the stabilizer. Apply the design to the base fabric by using a tiny zigzag bartack or stitching-in-the-ditch of the dart or tuck with monofilament thread.

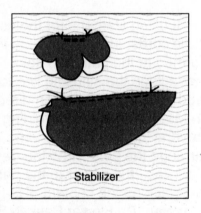

Stabilizer

SJR Tip To make a tuck in small flowers use a wide multi-stitch zig-zag bartack. Place the fold parallel to the needle swing; lower the feed dogs and stitch in place about three stitch cycles.

To finish the flowers, place a small square of Wonder Tape on the flower center. Stick the yarn end in the tape center and wind, around covering the tape; cut and tuck the yarn end under. Tack the yarn in place with free-motion machine stitches using a darning foot. Use this method for flowers and leaves in Chapters 8 - Spring Garden and 10 - Flower Basket; specific details are given for individual flower types.

SJR Tip Leave the flowers attached to the stabilizer after the tuck is stitched. Fold them open and apply the centers, then remove flowers from the stabilizer.

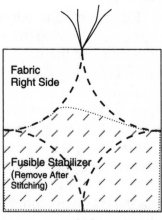
Method Four

Small flowers can be shaped from squares or circles by gathering the stitch pattern lines. Trace the design and stitch pattern onto the matte side of a fusible stabilizer, cut out pattern and fuse lightly to the suede <u>right side</u>. Cut out the design; <u>do not remove the pattern.</u> With monofilament thread in the needle and all-purpose thread in the bobbin, stitch (4mm length) following the stitching lines on the pattern. Remove the pattern and gather tightly; tie threads to secure. Wrap one of the thread ends around the stitching line, tie again.

Fabric Right Side

Fusible Stabilizer (Remove After Stitching)

If using stamens for the center (pieces of folded yarn, metallic cords, etc.) insert them into the cup formed at the gathered flower center and bartack on the stitching line to secure. If adding centers using the directions given in Method Three or by folding and tacking several inches of wispy yarn, open and arrange the petals into the desired position. Tack the flower to the base fabric and tack on the centers. (Use this method for flowers in Chapter 10 - Flower Basket. Specific details are given for individual flower types.)

Insert Stamens

Stitching Line

Chapter 4

Ribbon Flowers

Create grosgrain or double-faced satin ribbon flowers and leaves by simply folding, stitching and gathering. Use the ribbon flowers singly or with Ultrasuede flowers for more texture. These dimensional ribbon flowers and leaves are uncrushable when made from grosgrain ribbon.

Day Lilies Wall Hanging Or Pillow
Chapter 11

Large Flowers And Leaves

The technique for making large flowers and leaves includes folding, stitching and sometimes gathering a piece of ribbon to obtain the dramatic dimensional shape. Ribbons used for large flowers are 5/8" to 7/8" wide; leaf ribbons are 3/8"- to 7/8"- wide. For drama use wider, printed or non-conventional colors of ribbon!

Chapters 11 - Day Lilies and 14 - Poinsettia And Holly offer specific ribbon widths and lengths for large design projects. Chapter 10 - Flower Basket offers ribbon leaves used with Ultrasuede flowers.

Materials

- 5/8"- or 7/8"-wide grosgrain or satin ribbon for flower petals or frilly leaves
- 3/8"- or 5/8"-wide grosgrain or satin ribbon for tapered leaves
- Firm yarn or stamens for flower centers
- All-purpose thread to match ribbon
- Monofilament thread for tacking
- Tear-away stabilizer placed under the design area

Basic Petals or Frilly Leaves

Cut the ribbon petal or frilly leaf twice the finished length plus 1/2" to 3/4"; the extra length is gathered (more length equals fuller petal). Right sides together, fold each ribbon piece in half crosswise. Use a 4mm stitch length and matching thread. Stitch, starting and backstitching at the folded ribbon edge and continue stitching on a bias line (45º angle) to the long edge of the ribbon. With the needle down,

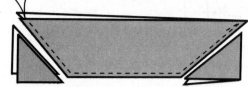

raise the presser foot and pivot, continuing to stitch along the long finished ribbon edge, pivot again. Stitch on the bias line, to the raw edges, <u>do not backstitch at this end</u> and leave a thread tail to pull. Trim both ends of the ribbon outside the stitching line and seal the raw edges with seam sealant.

Gather the petals <u>slightly</u> by pulling a thread end, tie threads to secure. Finger press the petal open.

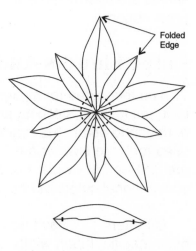

Folded Edge

The petals are attached to the base fabric with the folded edge to the outside. Secure the petals at the flower center with straight stitching or attach single leaves with a bartack at each end.

Use the frilly leaves with the small Ultrasuede flowers in Chapter 10 for texture. To make the leaves, cut the 5/8"-wide ribbon 5 1/2" to 8 1/2" long.

Tapered Leaves

For a long tapered leaf, with a smoothly tapered tip, cut a piece of 3/8"- to 5/8"-wide ribbon twice the desired finished length. Right sides together, fold ribbon in half crosswise. Stitch with a regular stitch length, starting and backstitching at the folded edge of the ribbon to the opposite side (30º angle). With the needle in the ribbon raise the presser foot and pivot, continuing to stitch along the long finished ribbon edge backstitching at the raw edge. Trim the folded end of the ribbon outside the stitching line and seal the raw edges with

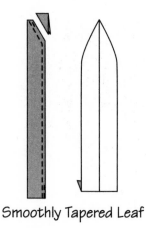

Smoothly Tapered Leaf

seam sealant. Finger press the leaf open and fold under the lower edge. Stitch the leaf center to the base using a small zigzag (1mm width and length) and invisible or matching machine embroidery thread.

To quickly make a tapered leaf, with a more angular tip, cut a piece of 3/8"- to 5/8"-wide ribbon twice the desired finished length. Right sides together, fold the ribbon in half crosswise. Stitch, starting and backstitching at the folded ribbon edge, along the finished edge, backstitch at the raw edge. Open the leaf turning the folded edge to the wrong side. While not as gracefully shaped at the tip as the previous leaf, this tip does not have to be tacked to conceal a raw edge.

Use these narrow leaves with the lilies in Chapter 11, or use them to add texture to the Ultrasuede flower design in Chapter 10.

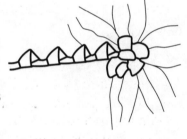

Fold

Quick Tapered Leaf

Flower Centers

For large ribbon flower centers use 1/2 yard of 1/4"-wide ribbon. Tie closely spaced knots in the ribbon. Machine tack the knots to the flower center, bunching them together and tucking the ribbon ends under.

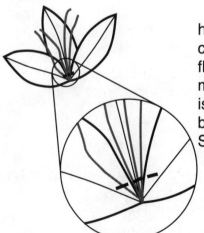

Other flowers, like lilies, may have only stamens added to the centers. In this instance, the flowers petals are attached and manipulated so that the center is not flat. The stamens are double lengths of firm cord or yarn. See page 53 for making lilies.

Lapel with Poinsettia and Holly Design Chapters 5 and 14

Notes:

Chapter 5
Detachable Lapels

These three detachable vest or jacket lapels attach with Soft & Flexible Velcro. They can be used singly (asymmetrically) or in pairs and embellished as desired. Instructions include a conventional construction method using a facing and an unfaced method for Ultrasuede. The lapels can also be cut from fabric highlighting a specific portion of the fabric design. The lapel patterns are found at the end of the chapter.

Chrysanthemums And Leaves Lapel
Chapter 9

Conventional Construction Method

With the conventionally faced construction method, the embellished lapel is made with the upper lapel and the lapel facing sewn right sides together along the outer edges, then turned and finished. The finished lapel is then folded along the pattern fold line and attached to the garment wrong side with Velcro.

Materials

- 3/8 yard of fabric cut on crosswise grain **or** 1/2 yard of fabric cut on lengthwise grain
- 1/3 yard of fusible interfacing
- 1/4 yard of pattern tracing cloth
- 1/4 yard of tear-away stabilizer
- 3/8 yard of 5/8"-wide Soft & Flexible Velcro for each lapel
- Thread to match lapel fabric

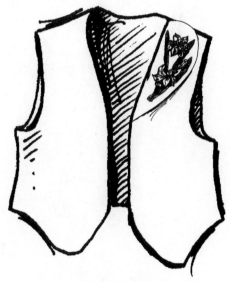

Day Lilies Lapel
Chapter 11

21

Conventional Cutting and Construction

Trace the desired lapel pattern onto pattern tracing cloth; matching the outer lines and the fold line on both pattern sections. Compare the lapel length to your garment neckline and shorten or lengthen along the pattern joining line as needed.

From the fashion fabric, cut two lapels; one is the upper lapel and one is the lapel facing. Cut one lapel from fusible interfacing and apply it to wrong side of one piece. Trim 1/8" off the outer edges of the remaining piece (lapel facing). Embellish the lapel so the embellishing stitches will not show on the finished lapel. Place tear-away stabilizer on the wrong side of the project during embellishing.

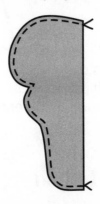

With right sides together, stitch the upper lapel outer edges to the lapel facing using a 1/4" seam allowance. Clip curves and turn the lapel right side out; press.

Press both layers under along the foldline. Clean-finish or serge the raw edges together.

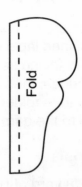

Fold

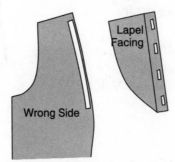

Lapel Facing

Wrong Side

Cut the Velcro loop strip slightly shorter than the front garment edge. Hand stitch the loop Velcro to the garment wrong side, 1/4" from the finished neck edge. Cut the Velcro hook strip into three or four equal pieces and machine stitch these pieces to the lapel facing under side.

To keep upper edge of the lapel against the garment, sew a small hook to the lapel facing corner and make a thread loop on the garment shoulder seam.

Unfaced Construction

Using the Ultrasuede construction method, a facing is not needed; the lapel is made from a single layer of Ultrasuede. Cut the pattern out of the suede then cut along the pattern fold line, creating a lapel piece and a facing strip.

Materials

- 1/4 yard of Ultrasuede cut on crossgrain **or** 1/2 yard cut on lengthwise grain
- 1/4 yard of pattern tracing cloth
- 1/4 yard of tear-away stabilizer
- 3/8 yard of 5/8"-wide Soft & Flexible Velcro for each lapel unit
- Thread to match lapel fabric

Cutting and Construction

Trace the desired lapel pattern onto the pattern tracing cloth matching the outer lines and the fold lines on both pattern sections. Compare the lapel length to your garment neckline and adjust as needed.

Cut one lapel from Ultrasuede, trimming the 1/4" seam allowance off outer lapel edges. Cut the lapel in two pieces, along the foldline. (Faux suede does not keep a sharply pressed fold, so this band will be sewn to the lapel during construction.)

Place tear-away stabilizer on the lapel wrong side and embellish the lapel as desired. Remove the stabilizer.

Wrong Side

With wrong sides together, use Wonder Tape to hold the facing strip to the lapel and edgestitch.

Apply the Velcro and the hook and eye according to Conventional Construction above.

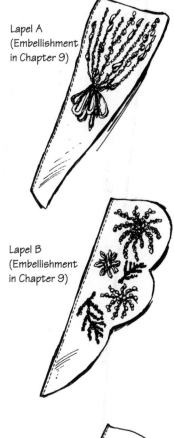

Lapel A
(Embellishment in Chapter 9)

Lapel B
(Embellishment in Chapter 9)

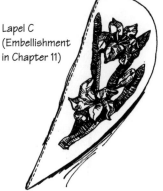

Lapel C
(Embellishment in Chapter 11)

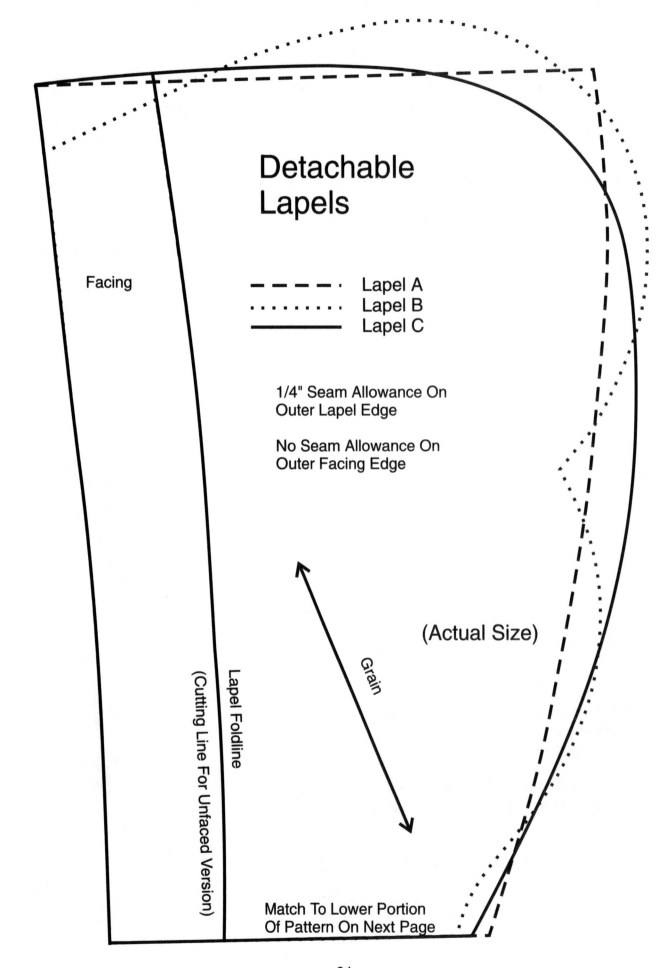

Detachable Lapels

- – – – – Lapel A
- · · · · · · Lapel B
- ——— Lapel C

1/4" Seam Allowance On
Outer Lapel Edge

No Seam Allowance On
Outer Facing Edge

Facing

(Actual Size)

Grain

(Cutting Line For Unfaced Version)

Lapel Foldline

Match To Lower Portion
Of Pattern On Next Page

24

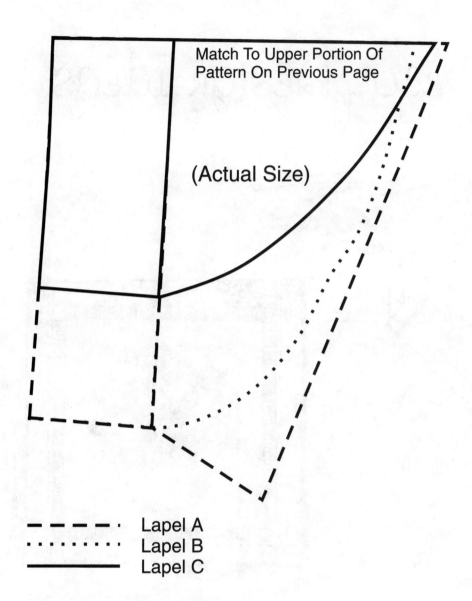

Match To Upper Portion Of
Pattern On Previous Page

(Actual Size)

- - - - Lapel A
· · · · · Lapel B
——— Lapel C

Home Decor Design Ideas

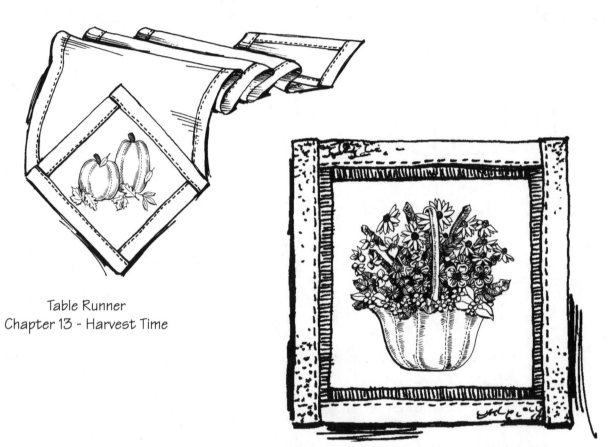

Table Runner
Chapter 13 - Harvest Time

Wall Hanging or Pillow
Chapter 10 - Flower Basket

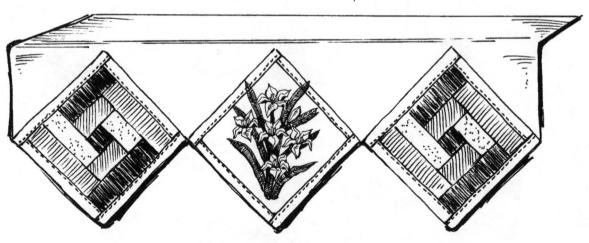

Mantle Scarf
Chapter 11 - Day Lilies

Chapter 6

Shirt Shawls

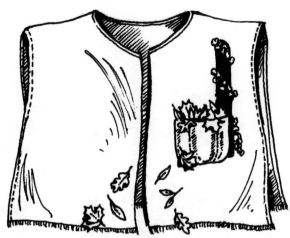

Harvest Time
Chapter 13

The shirt shawl is a terrific way to quickly make a garment to celebrate a holiday or special occasion. The shawl is a perfect canvas to try out many of the techniques or projects in this book. The basis for the shirt shawl is a good quality, basic color made-to-wear or a ready-to-wear shirt with a collar and collar stand. The secret is one shirt with many quick-to-make shawls! (See Photo 3, 16, and Front Cover)

Materials

- 1/3 to 1/2 yard of fabric to match or coordinate with the shirt or seasonal fabric
- 1 yard of pattern tracing cloth
- 1/2 yard of 5/8"-wide Soft & Flexible Velcro to attach the shawl to the shirt
- Embellishment materials of your choice

SJR Tip If you are making your shirt, purchase extra fabric for several shirt shawls.

Pattern Making

Ready-To-Wear Shirt

Using a ready-to-wear shirt, the shawl pattern will be traced directly from the shirt. Button up the shirt and lay it on a flat surface so it's folded at the top of the shoulder, regardless of where any yoke seams may be. Place a piece of pattern tracing cloth on one-half of the shirt upper half. Trace along the armhole seamline, across the shoulder 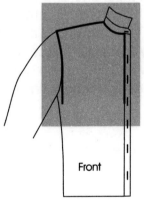 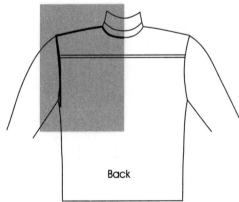 fold, around the bottom of the collar stand and down the inner edge of the front placket. Mark the shawl pattern at your bust point; this will be helpful in designing the lower shawl

Front

Back

27

edge and in determining the embellishment placement. To trace the shirt back, place a straight edge of the tracing material on the center back. Trace around the lower edge of the collar stand, across the shoulder fold and down the armhole seamline.

Made-To-Wear Shirt

With a made-to-wear shirt, trace the shawl pattern directly from the front and back pattern pieces. On the front, trace the seamline along the armhole, across the shoulder, along the neck and down 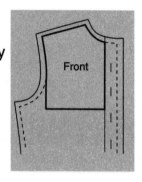 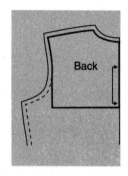 the placket edge. On the back place the straight edge of the tracing material along the center back, trace the seamline around the neck, across the shoulder and down the armhole. For a yoked pattern, pin the yoke to the front and back shoulder seam. Matching the underarm seams, fold at the shoulder. Trace the front and back pattern using the fold as the shoulder line.

Finishing

To the traced shawl pattern pieces add the following seam allowances: 1/4" along the neck edge and the shoulder line and 1/4" - 1/2" along the arm-hole. (The armhole is a slightly curved edge so a narrow hem or turned under edge is the best finish.)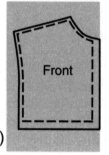

Harvest Time
Chapter 13

The lower edge of the shawl can change shape and length each time you make a new one. The front shawl should end slightly above or a couple of inches below the bust point.

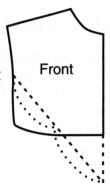 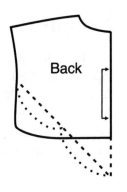

Front

Back

SJR Tip Curve the bottom outer edges up slightly to "hang" better on the body. Or use a deep V with the outer edges above the bust point and the center point below bust level. For a softer look scallop the edges.

The amount added to the front and lower edges depends upon the edge finish:

1. Add 1/4" for a decoratively serged edge. This will be trimmed during serging to give a nice smooth edge.
2. Add 1/2" for a narrow double-fold hem.
3. Add 1" for a wide hem. Miter the hem at the front corners.
4. Nothing is added if the edges are bound with bias tape or other trims, or if you take advantage of fabric with a fringed selvage (see Harvest Time Shawl, Photo 16).

Construction

Staystitch around the shawl neck edges. Serge or overcast all raw edges and stitch the shoulder seams.

Finish edges in the desired manner and embellish the shawl.

Edgestitch the Velcro loop strip to the bottom edge of the collar stand, beginning and ending at the outer front placket edges. It is important to stitch the Velcro loop strip to the shirt first.

Velcro Loop

Place the Velcro hook strip on the sewn-on loop strip and cut it to fit (it will be slightly longer because of the outward curve). Remove this strip and edgestitch the right side to the shawl seamline.

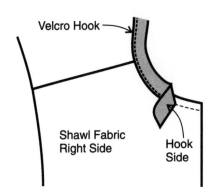

Velcro Hook

Shawl Fabric Right Side

Hook Side

Sculptured Shirt Shawl

To make the sculptured shirt shawl used in Chapter 8 - Spring Garden, enlarge the pattern in the grid below, adding a 1/4" seam allowance to the armhole area. Determine the appropriate finished length in center front and back and align the shawl pattern with the enlarged sculptured edge pattern. Curve the design side edges to blend with the pattern.

From the shaped shawl pattern, draft facings for the front and back lower edge and the armhole area. The facing should be 1 1/2" wide at the shoulder and 3" wide at the center front and back. The front facing will end at the front edge fold line.

Sew or serge the front and back facings together at the shoulder seam and clean finish the inner edges. Apply the facing to the shawl (1/4" seam allowance) instead of hemming the lower edges.

Celebrate with a shawl for each occasion! No one will know it's the same shirt.

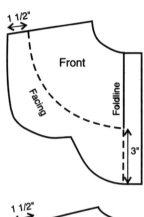

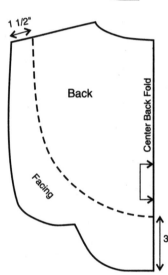

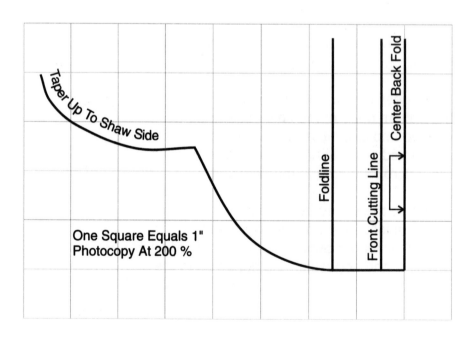

One Square Equals 1"
Photocopy At 200 %

30

Chapter 7

Cardinal's Roost

The brilliant cardinal perched on green pine is a delightful and cheery embellishment to enjoy all winter long. The finished design is approximately 11" square and fits a wall hanging, pillow or a garment (Photo 1). Ultrasuede is my first choice for the bird, but craft felt can be used with the same dimensional technique.

Materials

- 9" square of red suede or craft felt
- Black suede or felt scrap for cardinal's mask
- Yellow suede or felt scrap for cardinal's beak
- Black machine embroidery thread for eye and feet
- Brown Ribbon Floss, six-strand embroidery floss, soft cord or yarn for branches
- Two green 30-wt. machine embroidery threads for stitching pine boughs
- Monofilament invisible thread for applying cardinal
- Fusible stabilizer for pattern tracing
- 1/2 to 1 yard of crisp, firm tear-away stabilizer
- Fabric marker
- Wonder Tape
- Fusible interfacing for lightweight base fabric (optional)

SJR Tip To change the cardinal to a blue jay, use blue fabric and the jay head with the narrow beak. For a Steller's jay, use the jay head pattern cut from black fabric.

SJR Tip Use one or two layers of a crisp, firm stabilizer like Sulky's Stiffy behind the area to support the heavy stitching. If the base fabric is lightweight, fuse interfacing to the entire wrong side.

Pine

Using the fabric marker, draw in the main pine branches on the base fabric. Using the cardinal body pattern to help with placement. Place a piece of firm fabric stabilizer under the design area.

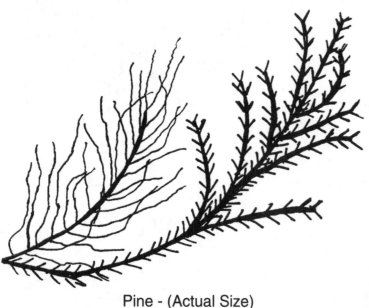

Pine - (Actual Size)

The pine branches are couched onto the base fabric. To couch, lay cord, yarn or floss in place on the base fabric and stitch over it with an embroidery or monofilament thread in the needle and bobbin or all-purpose thread in the bobbin. A variety of stitches can be used for couching depending upon whether it's decorative or merely functional.

Short Needle Pine

To form the short pine needle branches, thread the machine needle with the green embroidery thread and use a feather stitch to couch the floss or yarn. Use the widest stitch width and lengthen the stitch length, if necessary.

Long Needle Pine

To form the branch of the long needle pine, couch over floss or yarn with monofilament thread using a zigzag, with the stitch width spanning the floss. Use a small zigzag or lighting stitch to form the long needles. To achieve the illusion of depth, make some of the needles curve over the center branch.

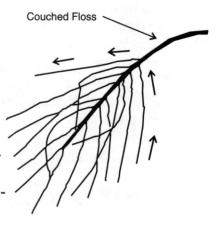

Couched Floss

SJR Tip

Look at the stitches on your machine, you may have other stitch options for forming the pine branches. For example, the stretch or lightning stitch (A-6) on Husqvarna Viking's # 1+ makes very realistic long pine needles. Use the first stitch on the E cassette to create cedar branches.

32

Cardinal

Trace the cardinal pattern onto the matte side of the fusible stabilizer. Make sure all the nap arrows are going in the same direction for shading dimension on the finished Ultrasuede design. Rough cut the pattern pieces and fuse them to the suede or felt wrong side. Cut out the pieces and remove the pattern. The cardinal will be assembled on the project after stitching the pine design.

For a front garment design, eliminate some of the pine branches and photocopy the cardinal pattern at 75%.

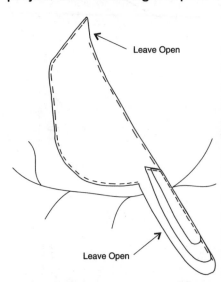

Leave Open

Leave Open

Use monofilament thread and a small zigzag or straight stitch, and stitch the cardinal body in place on the branches according to the stitching lines on the pattern pieces. Refer to page 15, Method Two, for stitching technique details. Place a small strip of Wonder Tape on the wrong side of each of the tail and wing pieces. Assemble the two tail pieces and place them on the body, stitching along the upper edge only.

Beginning with the largest wing, stitch each of the wing layers in place as indicated on the pattern. This diagram shows the Steller's jay variation.

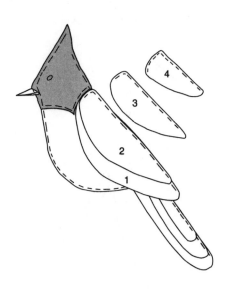

The beak and mask can be fused and/or stitched in place (for jays, use longer beak and no mask). Position the beak first; then the mask. Use black straight stitching or permanent marker for beak detail. Satin stitch the eye or attach a tiny black bead. Satin stitch (2mm wide) the legs as shown on the pattern on the next page. Clip into suede on unstitched crest. Remove the stabilizer.

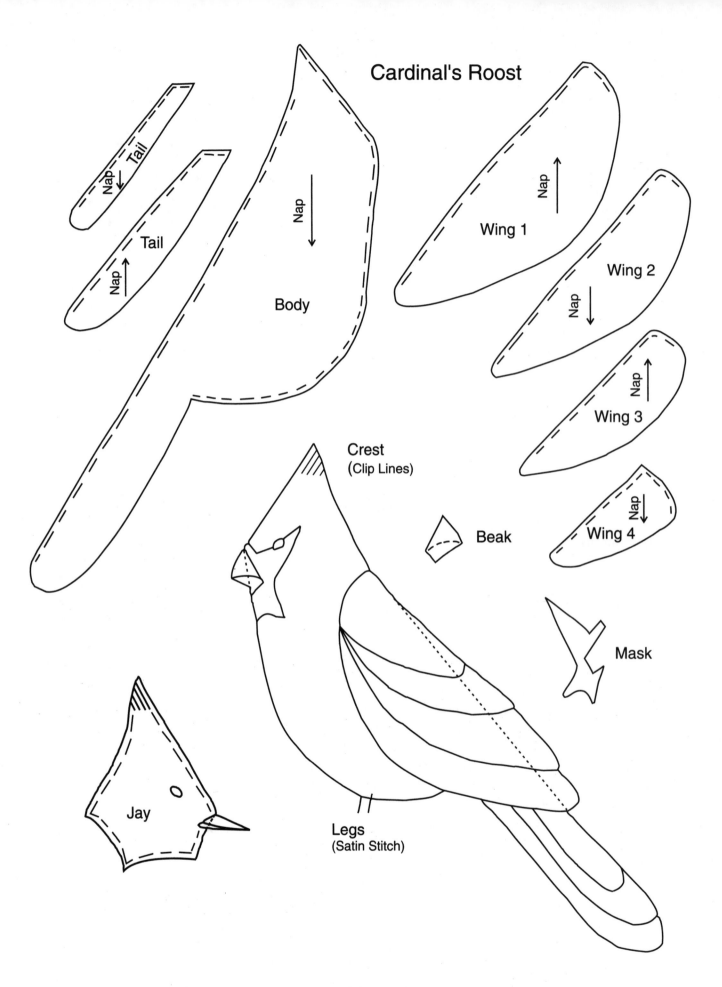

Cardinal's Roost

Tail
Nap

Tail
Nap

Body
Nap

Wing 1
Nap

Wing 2
Nap

Wing 3
Nap

Wing 4
Nap

Crest
(Clip Lines)

Beak

Mask

Jay

Legs
(Satin Stitch)

Photo 1

Photo 2

Photo 4

Photo 3

Photo 5

Photo 7

Photo 6

Photo 8

Photo 9

Photo 10

Photo 11

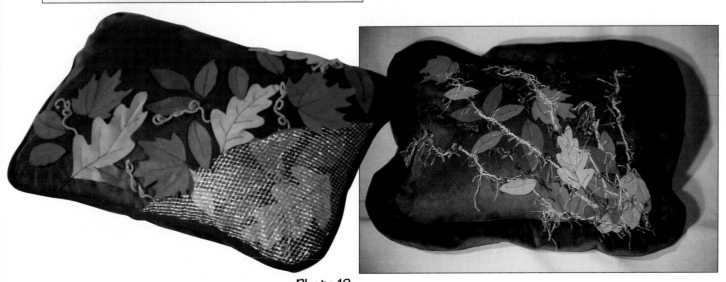

Photo 12

Photo 13

Photo 14

Photo 15

Photo 17

Photo 16

Photo 18

Chapter 8

Spring Garden

Spring showcases fuzzy pussy willow blossoms followed by the brightly colored flowers, including tulips, iris and tiny violets. With the inclusion of tucks and darts these flowers become realistically dimensional (Photos 2, 3 and Back Cover). Ultrasuede adapts best to these dimensional techniques; craft felt does not have enough draping qualities. The designs can be adapted for traditional appliqué by folding out the dart or tuck on the pattern and then cutting out the design.

Sculptured Shirt Shawl Back
Front Shawl Illustration on Page 39

Materials

- 1/2 yard fabric for sculptured edge Shirt Shawl (Chapter 6, Page 30) as a base
- Two squares or 1/8 yard of green Ultrasuede for the leaves and stems (two greens used in sample)
- One square or 1/8 yard of a light and a dark Ultrasuede for the iris petal combination
- One square or 1/8 yard of bright Ultrasuede for tulips
- One square or 1/8 yard of violet Ultrasuede
- 8" of chenille or other heavy yellow/gold yarn for iris beards (4" per flower)
- 1 yard of medium-weight yellow yarn for violet centers
- 1 yard of bulky chenille yarn for pussy willows
- Narrow brown Ultrasuede strips, ribbon floss or heavy yarn for pussy willow stems
- Seam sealant
- Monofilament and all-purpose (match design) thread
- Scraps of black and two other colors of Ultrasuede for butterflies
- Black machine embroidery thread for stitching butterflies
- Fusible stabilizer for tracing the pattern designs
- Tear-away stabilizer
- Wonder Tape for holding designs in position

> **SJR Tip**
> Ultrasuede or Ultrasuede Light can be used for these flowers, sometimes color is the deciding factor. Ultrasuede Light is softer and more petal like, but does crush and wrinkle quicker.

Basic Cutting and Construction

Refer to page 14, Dimensional Appliqué Basics, for tracing and cutting the flower petals and leaves. For the iris and tulip stems, cut 1/4"-wide Ultrasuede strips; if using Ultrasuede strips for pussy willow stems, cut 1/8" wide.

See page 15, Method Three, for stitching darts, tucks and violet centers.

After stitching the darts and tucks, arrange the flowers, stems and leaves in place on the base, using Wonder Tape or pins to hold the designs in position. Build depth into the design by intertwining the stems and leaves instead of creating separate layers. When the design is complete, remove the upper designs and stitch from the bottom layer up.

Individual flower and leaf assembly instructions follow.

Wall Hanging or Pillow

Leaves and Stems

Use monofilament thread and a straight stitch to apply the leaves to the base. Stitch in and out of the ditch. This winding stitch pattern will keep the leaves from folding up or requiring additional bartacks. For the long leaves, fold under 1" of the tip and stitch only to this fold.

Stitch the stems with a straight stitch along one edge, using either invisible or matching embroidery thread. Curve the stems slightly when stitching for a more natural look.

Iris

Cut two sets of each iris petal shown on page 37. Cut and stitch the darts in the iris petals. Bartack the center of the 4" yarn on the lower petal group center, 1/2" from upper edge.

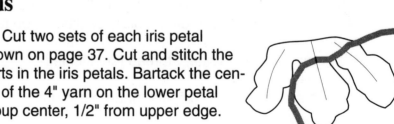

Tape this lower petal group in place over the stem and bartack both yarn ends together at the upper edge of the center petal. Form loops on both sides of the center. Tack these loops on the outer petals over the top end of the darts. Tack each yarn end to close the outer loops. The top petals will cover the cut ends of the yarn. Place a pencil or dowel crosswise under the three petals to add dimension, then tack each petal to the base at the end of the dart.

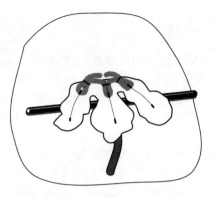

Tape the upper center petal to the base, with its lower edge covering the yarn ends. Stitch-in-the-ditch of the dart easing the petal to the base. Repeat for the two side petals, easing and curving them slightly for more shape and dimension.

Right Iris Petal

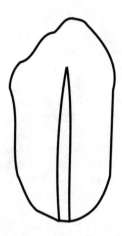

Center Iris Petal

Left Iris Petal

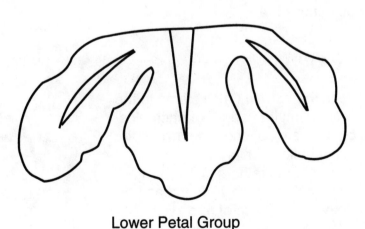

Lower Petal Group

37

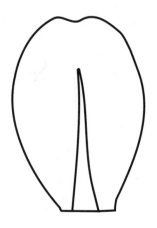

Tulip Petal

SJR **Tip** To get a feel for where the tulip should be positioned on the design, partially assemble and stitch it to a piece of stabilizer. Remove the stabilizer; turn the design right side up; and find its position on the base design. Stitch it again, in place on the base.

Tulip

Cut nine petals from the pattern at the left. Dart each petal. Place two petals, dart (wrong) side up, on the base with the petal top hanging down from the flower base position. With the darts towards the center, stitch between the darts 1/4" from the edge. Center the third petal on the first two, with the bottom edge slightly higher. Wrap the outer edges of the first petals over center petal edges and stitch them in place.

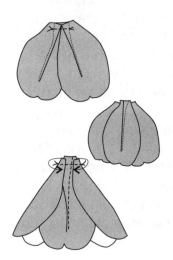

Fold the tulip petals so they are upright, with the right side of the Ultrasuede up. Place a small piece of Wonder Tape on the under side (Ultrasuede right side) of the outer two petals, use the tape to position the petals on the base fabric either as a flower in full bloom or in a tight opening bud.

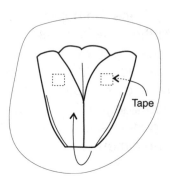

Fold back the upper petal edges and use bartacks to hold the outer and inner petals in place. It is a nasty thought but a hand-stitched bartack may be necessary!

Pussy Willow

Attach the narrow (1/8") stems to the base with a small zigzag. For each blossom cut a 1" strip of chenille yarn. (If the yarn is not bulky enough, use two strands twisted together.) Dab seam sealant on 1/4" of each yarn end and allow it to dry on a piece of non-stick paper. Use a multi-stitch zigzag to bartack one end of the yarn to the stem. Raise the presser foot and place the free end on top of the first and stitch

Seam Sealant

again. Trim yarn ends off close to the bartack and zigzag across the raw ends. Bartack the loop end to the base. Repeat for additional blossoms.

Violet

Cut fourteen violets and thirteen leaves from the pattern on the following page. Tuck or dart each piece and add centers to the violets (page 15, Method Three). Apply the leaves by stitching-in-the-ditch area of the dart. Partially hide some violets under the dimensional leaves and tack in place.

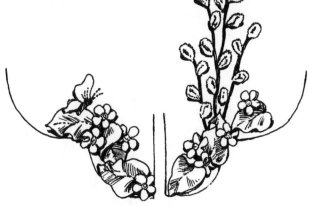

Shown On Sculptured Shirt Shawl Front

Butterfly

When the bright flowers bloom, the butterflies come to visit either flying through the blossoms or resting on a leaf or flower.

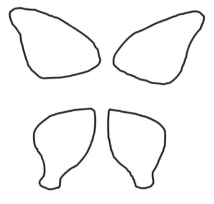

Butterfly Wings

Stitch the lower wing(s) on first, then the upper wing(s) following the stitching lines on the completed butterfly as a guide. The right and left set of wings should touch in the center. Edgestitch the body over the wing center or use a tapered satin stitch to make the body. The antennae are straight stitched beginning at the head to the desired length; backstitch one stitch and forward one stitch, repeated twice, for the antennae tip; then continue stitching back to the head.

Flying
Butterfly
Body

Resting
Butterfly
Body

SJR **Tip** This is a very dimensional technique! Let the project hang overnight so you can tell where additional small bartacks will be needed to hold the elements in place.

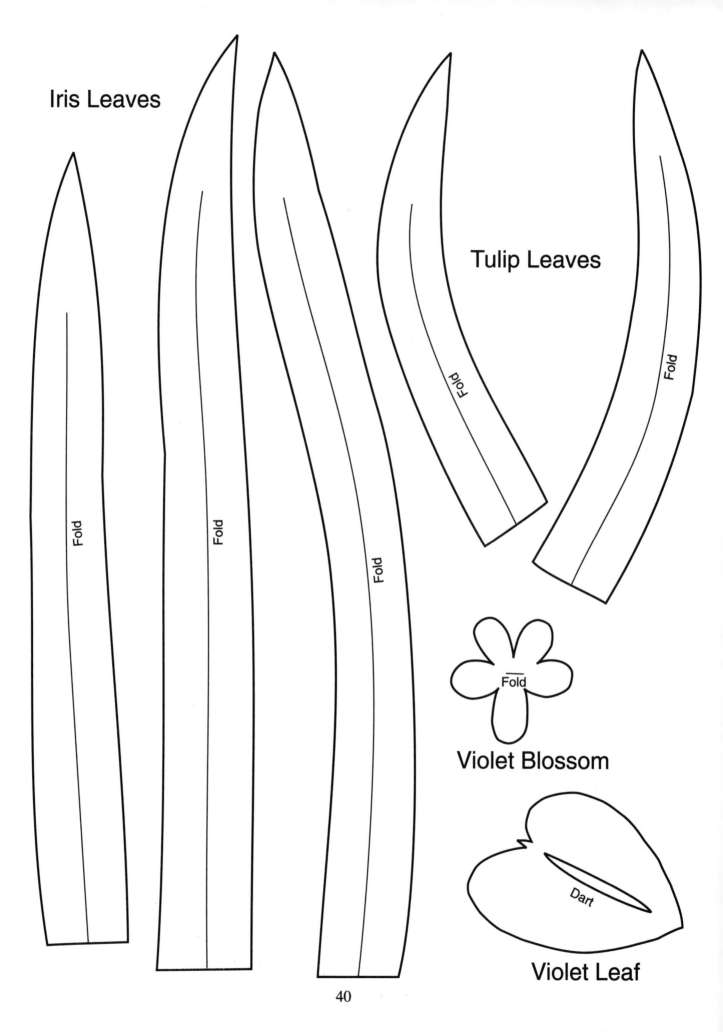

Iris Leaves

Tulip Leaves

Fold

Fold

Fold

Fold

Fold

Fold

Violet Blossom

Dart

Violet Leaf

Chapter 9

Stitch 'N Weave Designs

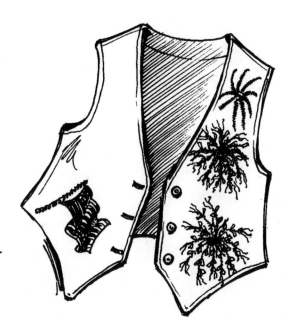

Choose one of the following designs to get you into the swing of the Stitch 'N Weave technique. Apply these designs to both ready-to-wear and made-to-wear garments to jazz up your wardrobe. (See Chapter 1 for the basic techniques.)

Fireworks Vest

The Stitch 'N Weave Fireworks celebrates our nation's birthday, New Years or any other special celebration. It's easy to do and gives a great splash of color! To help identify the celebration combine this design with Puff-liqué (Chapter 2). For the July 4th, a flag is waving in the breeze and a large, firecracker is about to explode. Notice in Photo 5 that the silver, Sulky Sliver stitching adds a bit of sparkle.

Materials

- Metallic machine embroidery thread
- All-purpose thread to match garment fabric
- Red and blue frizzy yarn
- 1/4 yard of flag or other print fabric appropriate for the occasion to Puff-liqué
- Water or air soluble marking pen or a permanent marking pen and water soluble stabilizer to transfer the design
- 1/2 yard of tear-away stabilizer
- Double-eye needle
- Small amount of fiberfill for Puff-liqué

Stitching and Weaving

Overlap the stitched lines in the starburst center. Photo 5 shows that the starbursts stitched with the metallic thread. The top one is stitched only, not woven.

Refer to page 9, Puff-liqué With Printed Fabrics. The vest flagpole is made from several metallic yarns couched together; the firecracker flame is gold metallic yarn secured with the firecracker stitching.

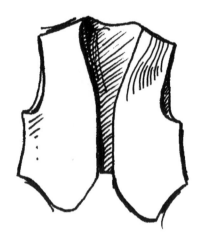

Scroll Placement

Shoulder Scroll Accent

The Stitch 'N Weave Shoulder Scroll is an upscale way to decorate a ready-to-wear jacket or vest and have some fun fooling your friends and colleagues! The tone-on-tone stitch pattern is a great but subtle embellishment to wear for awhile. Later for a change or when a busy schedule allows, weave yarns and ribbons through the stitching. The next season, change the yarn to the season's hottest color! Don't tell anyone it's the same garment! (See illustration on page 1 and Photo 8.)

Materials

- Machine embroidery and all-purpose thread to match garment fabric
- Assorted yarns
- 1/8"-wide satin ribbon for texture and color "punch"
- Water or air soluble marking pen or a permanent marking pen and water soluble stabilizer to transfer the design
- 1/4 yard of tear-away stabilizer
- Double-eye needle

Weaving

Shoulder Scroll features multiple yarn fringes or tails. Start weaving and backstitch to secure the yarn leaving a 1" to 1 1/2" tail; continue weaving a short distance and again secure the yarn with a backstitch; cut the yarn leaving another tail. Repeat the procedure.

Shield and Tassel Lapel

The Shield and Tassel is a Stitch ´N Weave design for Lapel A . Incorporate a tassel into the garment closure for a designer look (see Photos 14 and 18).

Materials

- Machine embroidery and all-purpose thread to match lapel fabric
- Assorted decorative yarns, cords or narrow ribbons
- Water or air soluble marking pen or a permanent marking pen and water soluble stabilizer to transfer the design
- 1/4 yard tear-away stabilizer
- Double-eye needle

Weaving The Tassel

Create the tassel loops during the weaving process and form a tassel (page 6).

Form "buds" by weaving short pieces of yarn with random large nubs from both ends (page 5).

SJR Tip A quick way to transfer Stitch 'N Weave designs is to trace the design onto water soluble stabilizer with a permanent marking pen and pin to fabric right side. Stitch and remove stabilizer.

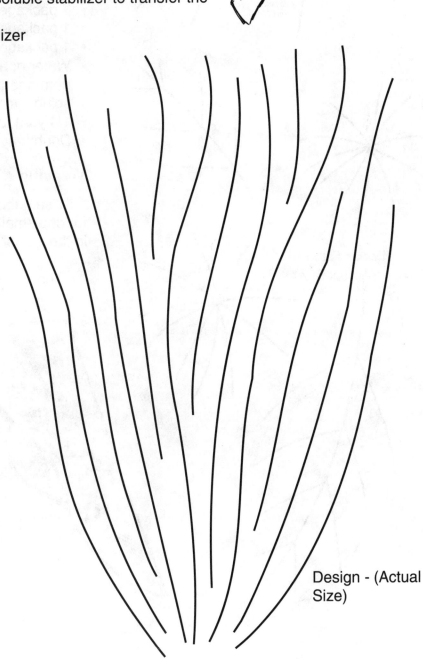

Design - (Actual Size)

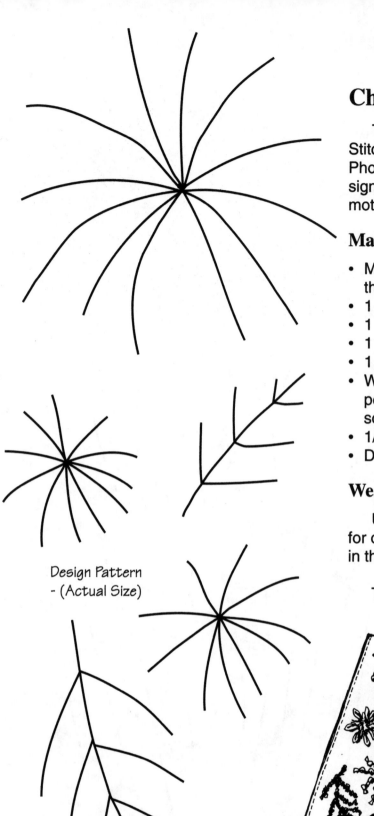

Design Pattern
- (Actual Size)

Chrysanthemum Lapel

The Chrysanthemum Lapel is a Stitch ´N Weave design for Lapel B (see Photo 13 and Back Cover). For this design the machine stitching overlaps in the motif center.

Materials

- Machine embroidery and all-purpose thread to match lapel fabric
- 1 package of nubby yarn
- 1 package of 4mm-wide silk ribbon
- 1 package of variegated chenille yarn
- 1 package of green chenille yarn
- Water or air soluble marking pen or a permanent marking pen and water soluble stabilizer to transfer the design
- 1/4 yard tear-away stabilizer
- Double-eye needle

Weaving

Use nubby yarns to create the petals for one small mum and fluff the yarn ends in the center (page 5).

The other small mum is backstitched with narrow silk ribbon (page 6).

Weave the large variegated mum and leaves with chenille yarn; pulling out, pinching and twisting small loops (page 5).

Chapter 10

Flower Basket

This Flower Basket project is designed to give you many flower options that can easily be used on smaller projects shown in the side margin illustrations and in Photos 9 and 10. The suede flowers are cut and manipulated or stitched and gathered to appear realistically dimensional. Leaf options include using the faux suede or ribbon to add texture. The finished project is approximately 14" square.

Combine these flowers with the Spring Garden flowers (Chapter 8) for other projects. Use a copy machine to reduce or enlarge the flower sizes depending upon the application. To acquire additional flower patterns, take apart silk flowers or even real flowers and trace their shapes. Patterns are at the chapter end.

Materials

- 1/4 yard of basketweave fabric
- 1/3 yard of large cord (#200) for basket handle
- 1/4 yard of Fusible Fleece™ for basket
- 1/4 yard of water soluble stabilizer for basket
- Squares of different color Ultrasuede or Ultrasuede Light for flowers and leaves
- 3/8"- to 5/8"-wide ribbon for leaves
- A variety of yarns for flower centers or firm cords for stamens
- Fusible stabilizer for patterns
- Monofilament thread for needle
- All-purpose thread for bobbin

Basket

The dimensional basket uses the Puff-liqué With Fleece technique (page 10). Use the pattern to cut the three fleece layers. The first layer is the basket and rim; the second layer is the basket's three center sections and rim; the third is basket center section and rim. Fuse the fleece layers together and insert then into the basket.

To make the basket handle cut two fabric strips 1 1/2" wide by 9" long on the lengthwise grain. Use the bias piecing technique to join the strips together at one end. Fold the strip lengthwise, wrong sides together. Stitch the strip long edges together using a 1/4" seam allowance; and turn right side out, inserting the cording in one end of the strip.

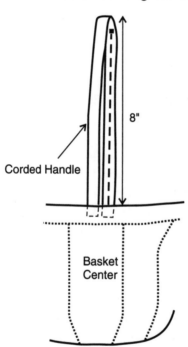

Corded Handle

8"

Basket Center

Use a small zigzag and monofilament thread in the needle to stitch the basket to the base fabric along the interior lines. With the corded end of the basket handle on top and the flat end offset underneath, place the handle ends under the top basket rim. Straight stitch up the center flat portion of the handle securing it to the base; bartack close to the handle fold. Stitch around the basket exterior with a blind hem stitch. Apply the desired flowers and leaves to finish the design. To add depth to a wall hanging design attach flowers and leaves to the back of the corded handle.

Ultrasuede Flowers and Leaves

To make these Ultrasuede flowers and leaves, follow Dimensional Appliqué Basics (page 14). The patterns are found at the end of this chapter. Add the violets and leaves from Chapter 8 if desired.

SJR Tip When using the basket design on a garment, the size may need to be decreased. To keep the design from being too stiff, omit the first layer of fleece.

SJR Tip Keep all those small flowers and leaves together (or from getting lost) by using a 6"-wide strip of stabilizer as a base for stitching darts and tucks. The flower centers could also be added at this time.(HTC's perforated Easy Stitch tears away in all directions making it especially easy to remove.)

Tucked and Darted - Flowers and Leaves

Use stitching Method Three (page 15) for primrose and lobed leaves. The following flowers use variations of this method.

Daisy/Coneflower/Black-Eyed Susan

For the daisy and black-eyed Susan, place two daisy pattern pieces right sides up staggering the petals. Fold right sides together and bartack with a multi-stitch zigzag close to the fold through all four layers. Open the flower and attach the yarn center to flower right side.

Make a coneflower by folding one design in half, wrong sides together, bartack and apply the yarn center over the folded edge.

Leaves

For leaf variety cut the lobed leaves with the rotary pinking blade or pinking shears; cut the violet leaves from Chapter 8 (Page 40) using a rotary wave cutting blade.

Shirt Collar
Primrose & Lobed Leaves

Stitched and Gathered Flowers

Follow the Dimensional Stitching Techniques - Method Four (page 16) for these flowers. Use a rotary pinking blade or wavy blade to cut fluted flowers edges, if desired.

Cyclamen/Columbine

Form these flowers by gathering the curved stitching pattern on a square, they can then be manipulated into different shapes. Two size squares are available to make a mature flower and an opening bud of Cyclamen/Columbine with the petals pointing upward. Other flowers could be opened flat with a yarn center or round-off corners for a different appearance.

Poppies

The poppy or other flowers with large centers are formed by gathering along the star stitched pattern in the circle. Make some circles 1/4" smaller for size variety. Wispy yarns make great poppy centers while smoother yarns are used for other flowers types. Remember the flowers should have eye appeal, not necessarily a carbon copy of nature.

Bachelor's Button/Carnation/Mum

To make bachelor's buttons and small mums use a rotary pinking cutter to cut 2" diameter circles; stitch along the stitching line and remove the pattern. Cut slashes radiating around the stitching line as shown on the pattern. Do not cut through stitching line. Gather and tie threads to secure.

To make a larger mum or carnation use the 2 1/2"-diameter circle; cut, slash and gather the mum as previously directed. Slash the carnation so it has wider petals as shown on the 2 1/2" circle.

Buds

To make "just-opening" buds to accompany the poppy or other flowers, cut 2" diameter circle with scissors or a wavy rotary cutter. Stitch, remove the pattern and gather. If desired, yarn can be inserted into the bud center.

Ribbon Leaves

Ribbon leaves can be added to the Ultrasuede flowers for added texture. Use the instructions on page 18, Basic Petals And Frilly Leaves and for the quick tapered leaves on page 19.

Flower Basket

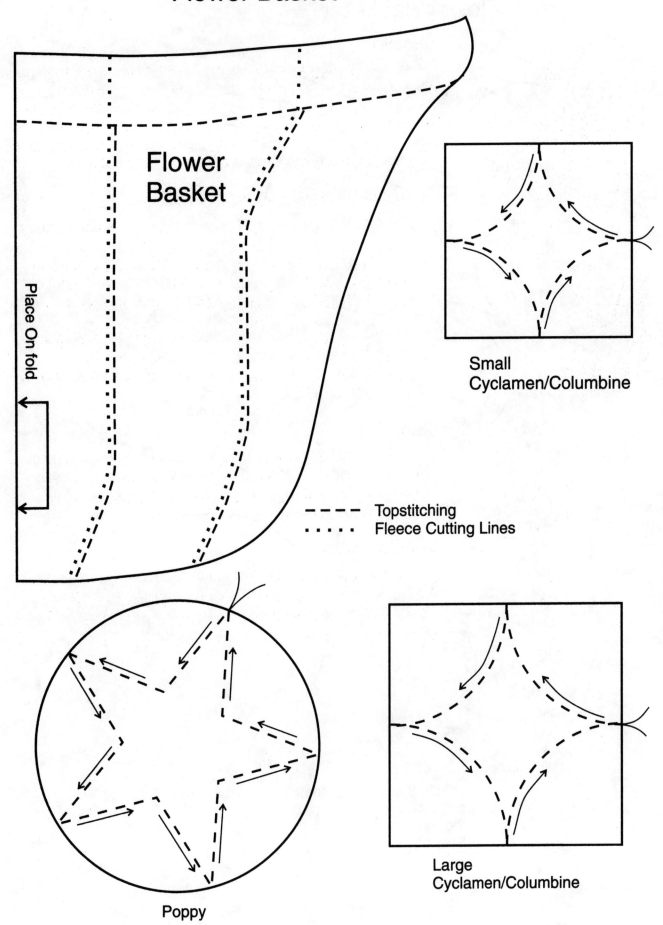

Flower
Basket

Place On fold

Small
Cyclamen/Columbine

- - - - Topstitching
· · · · Fleece Cutting Lines

Poppy

Large
Cyclamen/Columbine

Flower Basket

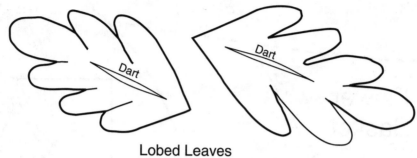

Lobed Leaves

Daisy

Primrose

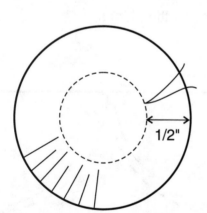

Buds
(Bachelor's Button
and Mum Slashes)

1/2"

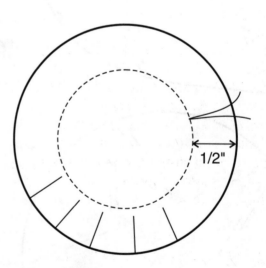

1/2"

Mum
(Carnation Slashes)

NOTE: Slash around the
entire circumference using
the slash pattern for the
flower type.

Chapter 11

Day Lilies

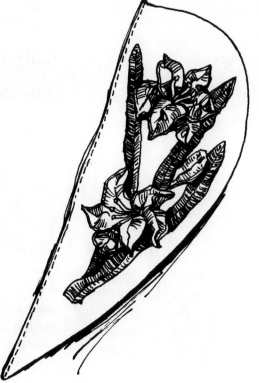

These bright and sunny summer flowers blossom when made with grosgrain ribbon. This ribbon allows them to be very dimensional and resilient. They're a great clothing embellishment on the detachable lapel, and also wonderful for pillows and wall hangings. (See Photos 15 and 17)

Materials

The materials given first are for the lapel design; in parentheses are the amounts for one flower or bud so you can adapt the yardages to the number of flowers your project requires. (See Chapter 5 - Detachable Lapels, for lapel pattern.)

- 1 2/3 yards (7/8 yard) of 5/8"-wide grosgrain ribbon for lilies
- 1 1/2 yards (5/8 yard) of 3/8"-wide grosgrain ribbon for leaves
- 1/3 yard (6") of a very firm cord like velour yarn or Ultrasuede cord for stamens
- 1/4 yard of 1"-wide grosgrain ribbon for bud
- 1/4"-wide ribbon for optional stems (Lapel has leaf placement so stems are not needed.)
- Thread to match ribbons
- Seam sealant

Note: Directions are given for the lapel. The wall hanging or pillow illustrated on page 17 has five lilies, one bud and seven leaves.

Lily Lapel

Lily Bud and Leaves

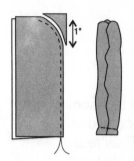

For each bud, cut the 1"-wide ribbon into three 2 1/2" long strips. Stitch two strips together, beginning in the ribbon center 1/8" down from the raw edge, gradually curving out to ribbon edge; continue stitching down the long edge of the ribbon. Repeat, stitching the third ribbon to the first two. Trim the ribbon along the curve and use seam sealant on all cut edges; turn bud right side out. Bunch the sides together at the open end and secure them together with a few hand stab stitches. Anchor the bud raw edge under the center stitching of a leaf in the next step and hand tack the bud top edge to the lapel.

For the leaves, cut two pieces of ribbon 16" long and one piece 20" long. Follow the instructions for the smoothly tapered leaf, page 18.

Flowers

For each lily, cut the 5/8"-wide ribbon into two 4 1/2" long strips, two 5" long strips and two 5 1/2" long strips. Follow the stitching directions in Basic Petals Or Frilly Leaves, page 18.

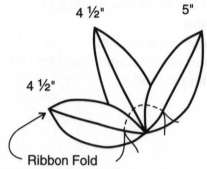

4 ½"   5"

4 ½"

Ribbon Fold

To attach the petals to the base fabric, first position one of the short petals with two of the smaller petals overlapping it on either side. Stitch between the seamlines of the outer petals.

For each flower's stamens, cut two 2 1/2" pieces of cord or yarn. Fold both stamens in half and position them together on top of the three petals. Lower the feed dogs and bartack them with a multi-stitch zigzag.

SJR Tip For additional detail, dip the stamen tips into black fabric paint or color with a permanent marking pen and allow to dry.

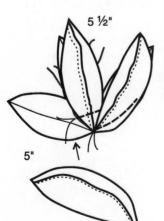

5 ½"

5"

Pin one of the long petals wrong side up on top of the stamens and stitch across the lower end. Pin the remaining two petals, wrong side up, overlapping the previous petal. Stitch these two petals on an angle. Fold down these three petals so they are right side up.

Arrange the petals puffing them up in the center of each petal. Lower the feed dogs and bartack (1.5mm width) the petal points in place.

53

Notes:

Chapter 12

Cascading Leaves

Celebrate nature with a graceful design of cascading leaves in either the traditional fall colors or those of your choice. For additional leaf shapes, go to the source – the trees in your yard or nearest park. Leaves can be made of faux suede or craft felt and applied by topstitching the vein lines or they can be applied using fabric and the Puff-liqué method (page 7).

Use spirals of thread or yarn to add additional texture to your design. Couch or tack on wispy thread to simulate a bare tree or bush, applying the leaves as if they were caught in the branches. Beads can be included for additional texture and shine. Metallic mesh fabric can add a bit of sparkle to your design as a see-through leaf container (Photo 12). For a more traditional look use a basket weave print to contain your leaves as shown on the Front Cover.

Any number or combination of leaves can be used depending upon the project and the base used. For most projects, use a mix of sizes and types of leaves. (Refer to Chapters 2 - Puff-liqué or 3 - Dimensional Appliqué for more details on the techniques.)

Leaf Pillow With Spirals
And Mesh Fabric

Suede or Felt Leaves

Materials

- Faux suede or craft felt scraps of in three to four different colors
- Black or brown 30-wt. machine embroidery thread
- Tear-away stabilizer
- Decorative threads or yarns, beads, metallic mesh or other specialty fabrics

Tie Beads Into Design
With Silk Ribbon

Cutting and Construction

Refer to page 14, Dimensional Appliqué Basics for tracing and cutting the leaves. Arrange the leaves in a pleasing design, overlapping them for a natural look. Pin or Wonder Tape leaves in place.

Decide where spirals, yarn or other accents will be stitched. If these are placed <u>under</u> the leaves they must be stitched first. (Photo 6)

Straight stitch (3 - 4mm length) the leaves to the base with the embroidery thread. Stitch along the vein lines, following the arrows on the leaf pattern. To form the stems, backstitch several times at the leaf end. Secure the thread ends on the back and remove the stabilizer.

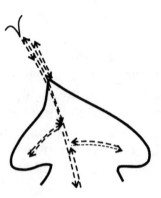

Puff-liqué Leaves

Materials

- Scraps of small prints or solid cotton fabrics in three or four different colors
- Water soluble stabilizer
- Fiberfill
- All-purpose thread to match fabrics
- Black or brown machine embroidery thread (30-wt.)
- Monofilament invisible thread

Cutting and Construction

For Puff-liqué it is necessary to simplify the maple leaf design. Refer to page 8, Puff-liqué Basics for cutting and constructing the leaves.

Cascading Leaves

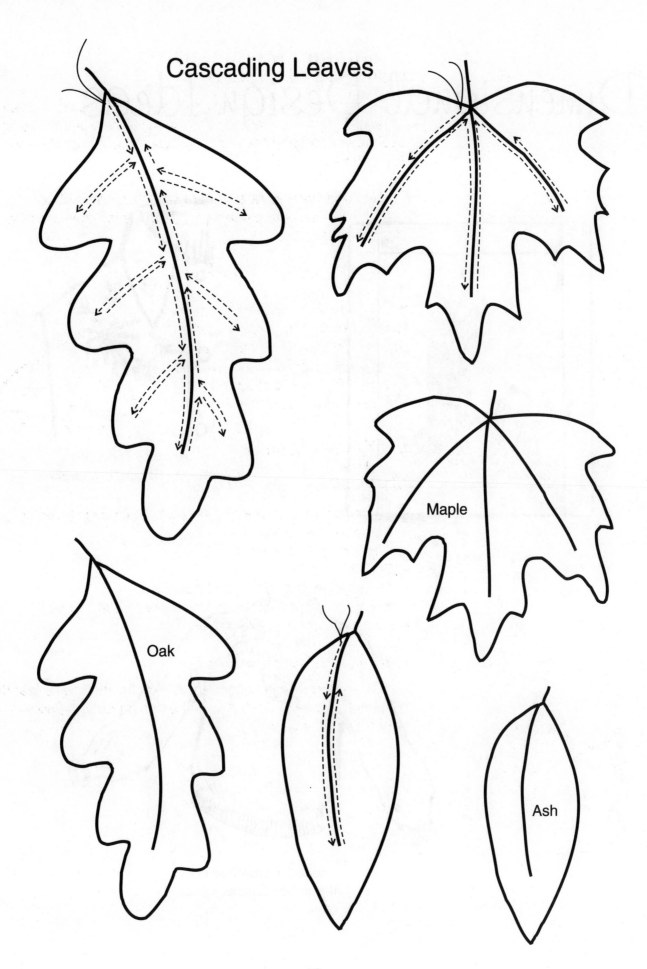

Maple

Oak

Ash

Dimensional Design Ideas

Wall Hanging Or Pillow
Chapter 13 - Harvest Time

Accents For A Shirt
Chapter 9 - Stitch "N Weave Designs

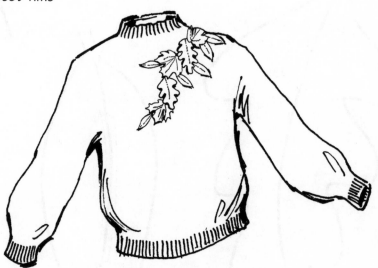

Sweater Embellishment
Chapter 12 - Cascading Leaves

Chapter 13

Harvest Time

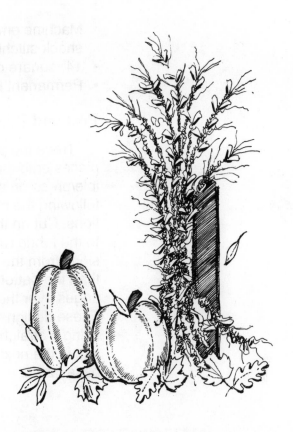

Harvest Time is displayed in a blend of traditional fall variety of techniques and textures. The pumpkins and basket can be made from cotton fabric, craft felt or Ultrasuede Puff-liqué. The corn shock is a Stitch 'N Weave design. Other design components are the suede or felt leaves, the post and pumpkin stems without the traditional appliqué satin stitch. The finished design is approximately 12"x12". (Technique details can be found in Chapters 1 - Stitch 'N Weave, 2 - Puff-liqué and 3 - Dimensional Appliqué.)

The following instructions are for the techniques used on the shirt shawl in Photo 16 and on the cover. Other options for design variations are given at the chapter end.

Materials

- 1/4 yard of "mottled," pumpkin color fabric for the pumpkins
- 1/4 yard of fabric for basket
- Green and brown fabric scraps of for stems and post
- Three colors of Ultrasuede or craft felt scraps for leaves
- Variety of novelty yarns, ribbons etc. for weaving corn shock
- Double-eye needle
- 1/2 yard of water soluble stabilizer
- 1/4 yard of fleece (fusible is optional)
- 1/8 yard of fusible/press-on appliqué backing, like APPLIQ-Ease
- Water soluble marking pen or other transfer pen
- Monofilament thread for outline appliqué
- Brown machine embroidery thread for pumpkin shaping and leaf veins

- Machine embroidery thread to match base fabric for corn shock stitching
- 14" square of tear-away stabilizer
- Permanent ink marker

Post and Pumpkin Stem Pieces

Trace the post and pumpkin stem pieces onto the paper side of the fusible/press-on appliqué backing, following the manufacturer's instructions. Cut on the design lines and fuse to the fabric wrong side. Cut the designs from the fabric a scant 1/4" larger than the pattern designs. Fold the raw edges over the appliqué backing edge and finger press. These designs are stitched in place with invisible thread using a straight or blind hem stitch. Use the corn shock tracing, in the next step to determine post placement on the base fabric.

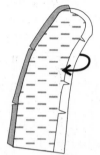

Corn Shock

Trace the complete corn shock design with a permanent ink marker onto a 8"x12" piece of water soluble stabilizer. After the post has been stitched onto the base fabric, pin the corn shock design on the water soluble stabilizer in place on the right side of the base fabric. Stitch along the traced solid lines using the ladder and/or blanket stitches. Tear off most of the water soluble stabilizer; use water to remove the remainder before continuing with the design. The weaving is done after all the other design elements are completed.

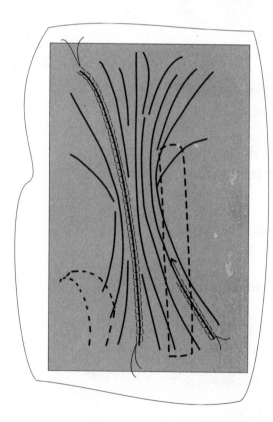

Pumpkins

For the pumpkins use the Puff-liqué With Fleece technique, page 10. The tall pumpkin has two layers of fleece in its center. The short pumpkin has one layer in the center and 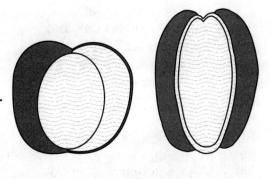 left side (finished view) and an additional layer in the center. Stitch the stems in place then straight stitch (3mm length) the pumpkin's interior lines with machine embroidery thread; stitch the outer pumpkin edges with invisible thread and a blind hem or straight stitch.

Leaves

Trace the leaves onto the matte side of fusible stabilizer and fuse the stabilizer to the suede or felt wrong side. Cut out the leaf designs; remove the stabilizer (reuse the pattern to make additional leaves). Stitch the leaves, with embroidery thread, along the vein lines and add stitched stems. The maple leaf can have added dimension using the Method One stitching technique, page 14.

Post

Repeat the procedure on the previous page for the post and apply it to the base fabric. Use one of the stitches recommended for the corn shock to stitch the vine over the post. The weaving will be done after the other design elements are completed.

Basket

For the basket use the Puff-liqué With Fleece technique, page 10. The basket has a layer of fleece plus a second layer in the center.

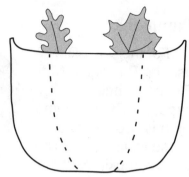

Place a piece of stabilizer under a maple and an oak leaf, stitch the vein lines with brown embroidery thread; remove the stabilizer. Tuck these two leaves, <u>wrong</u> side up under the upper edge of the basket. Stitch the basket to the base along the interior lines with either a straight stitch and embroidery thread (for plain fabric) or a 1mm length and width zigzag and invisible thread (for basket print fabric). Stitch the outer basket edges with invisible thread and a blind hem stitch, catching the two leaves in the stitching.

Tack the two leaves over the basket upper edge. Play with the other leaves' placement to make a basket full, stitching them to the base fabric. And of course, there are a few that drift out!

Remove all stabilizer material and weave the post vine.

See Chapter 1 - Stitch 'N Weave to weave the corn shock. To blend colors, weave from one row of stitching to another, side to side, as you weave up the shock. Do the darker yarns first and highlight with the lighter ones. Backstitch occasionally to anchor the yarn strands and loops. Fuzzy yarn with ribbon "flags" fills in quickly. (See Photo 16) Any yarn or mixture of yarns combined with bits of 4mm silk ribbon will give the same effect.

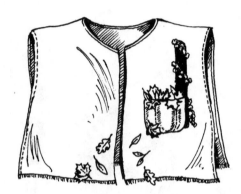

Technique Variations

The post, pumpkins, stems and basket can be made from Ultrasuede or craft felt. For the pumpkins and basket use the Ultrasuede or felt Puff-liqué variation, page 11. Use invisible stitching (invisible thread and a blind hem stitch) for the outer design edges.

The vine on the post can be a decorative machine stitch or hand stitching. The corn shock can be stitched with various decorative machine stitches along the design lines, adding additional stitched layers on top, shading with various thread colors for the different stitched lines. Test this on a sample!

Harvest Time

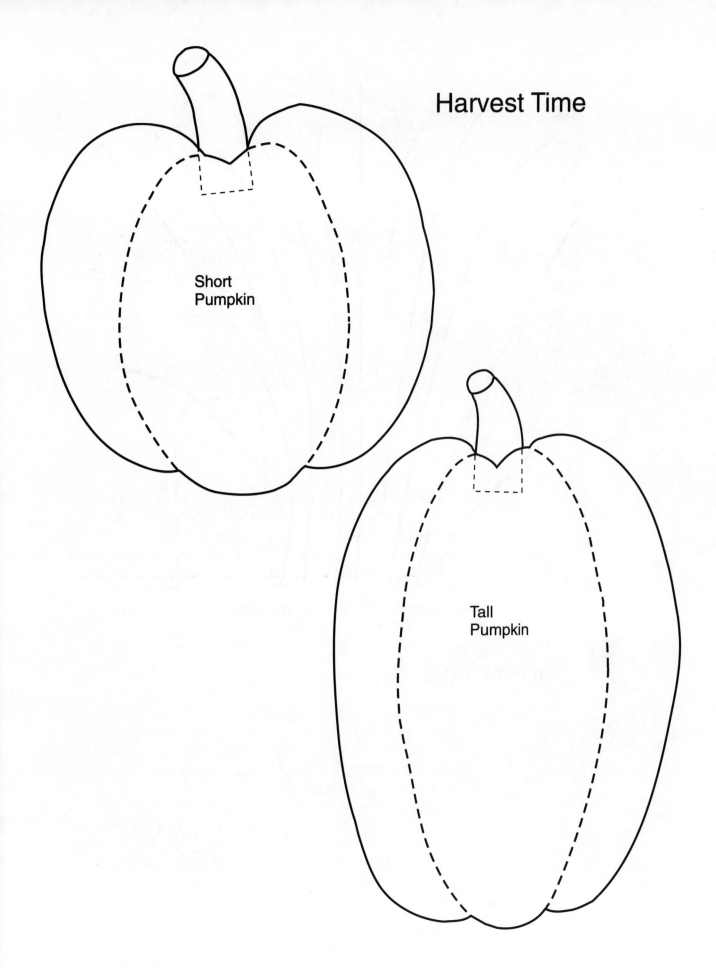

Short
Pumpkin

Tall
Pumpkin

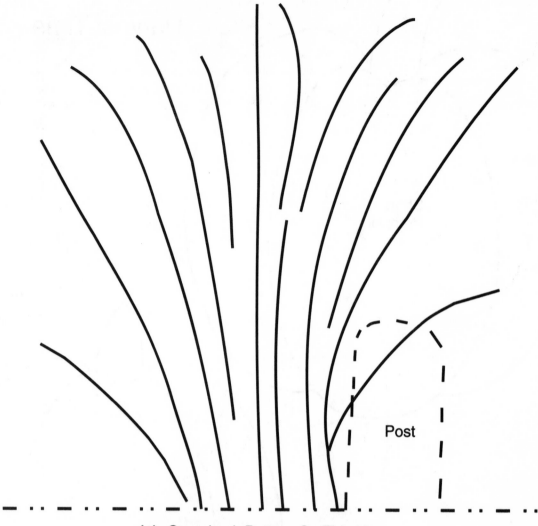

Post

Join Cornshock Pattern On This Line.

Harvest Time

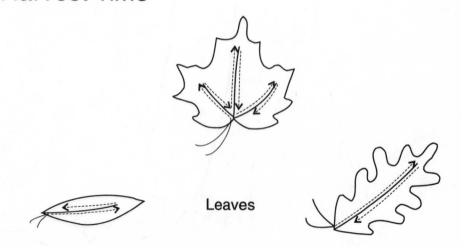

Leaves

Harvest Time

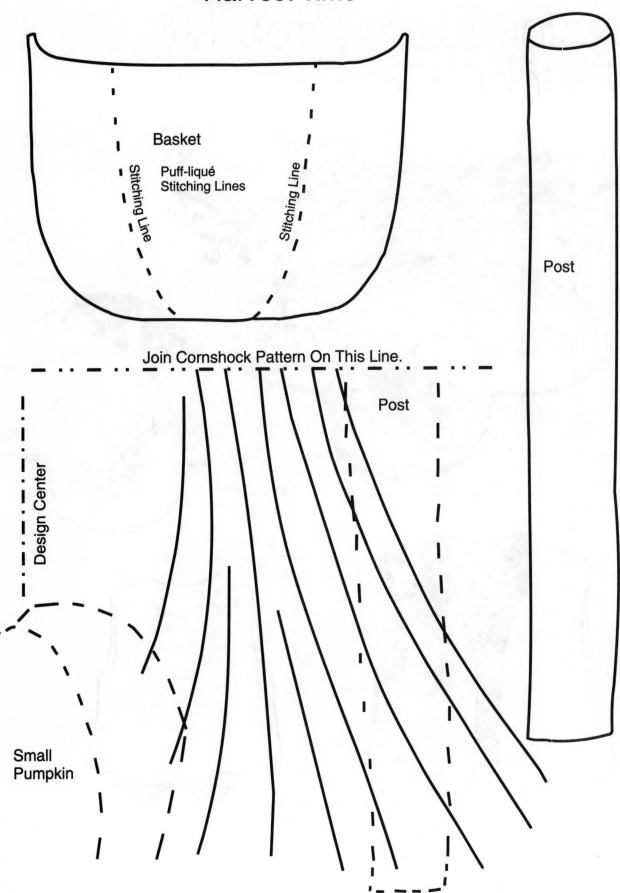

Basket

Puff-liqué
Stitching Lines

Stitching Line

Stitching Line

Post

Join Cornshock Pattern On This Line.

Design Center

Post

Small
Pumpkin

65

Design Ideas For The Holiday Season

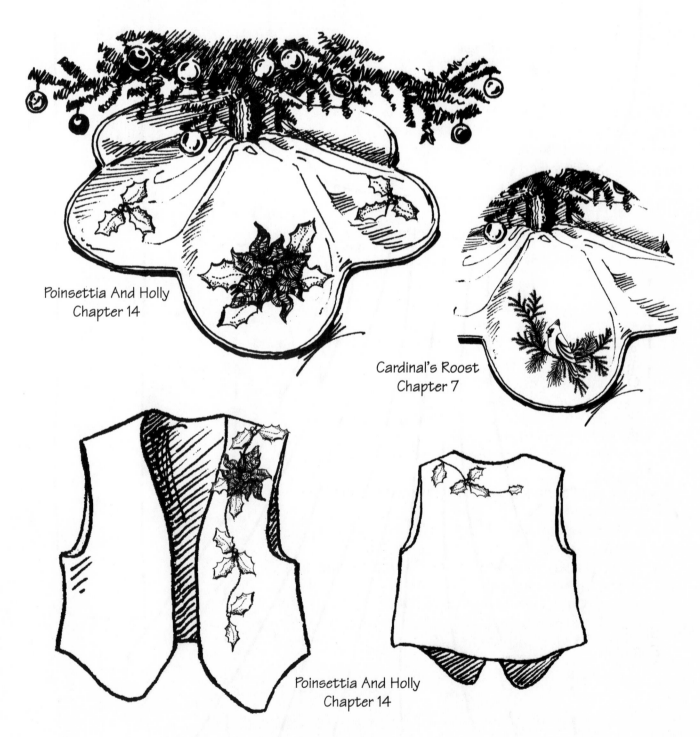

Poinsettia And Holly
Chapter 14

Cardinal's Roost
Chapter 7

Poinsettia And Holly
Chapter 14

Chapter 14

Poinsettia And Holly

This project combines Ultrasuede appliquéd holly leaves with a grosgrain ribbon poinsettia enhanced with berry buttons. Use this design on a vest, jacket or sweatshirt with the holly circling around the neckline. Make a Christmas tree skirt, pillow or wall hanging. (See Photo 4 and Back Cover)

Materials

- 1 1/8 yards of 7/8"-wide red grosgrain ribbon for large poinsettia petals
- 7/8 yard of 3/4"-wide red grosgrain ribbon for small poinsettia petals
- 1/2 yard of 1/4"-wide gold metallic or yellow satin ribbon for poinsettia center
- 1/8 yard or 9" square of green Ultrasuede for holly leaves
- 1 1/4 yard of dark green cord (twisted or rattail) for holly stem
- Eight 3/8"-diameter ball buttons for holly berries
- Red all-purpose thread for the poinsettia
- Black, gold or variegated metallic machine embroidery thread for holly leaf veins
- Monofilament invisible thread for couching stems and tacking the petals
- Fabric marking pen
- Seam sealant
- Fusible or tear-away stabilizer

Stems

Use the fabric marker to mark the stem placement. Apply seam sealant to the cord cut ends to prevent fraying. Pin the cord stem in place and couch it to the fabric base using monofilament thread, a cording foot and a machine zigzag or blind hem stitch.

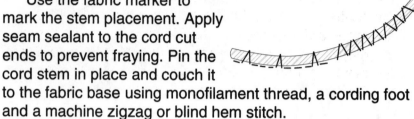

Poinsettia

Cut the 7/8"-wide ribbon into five pieces approximately 7" to 8" in length (Nature is not exact so why should we be?) Cut the 3/4"-wide ribbon into five pieces approximately 5" to 6" in length. The finished poinsettia is approximately 6" in diameter.

To make the poinsettia petals, follow the instructions for Basic Petals or Frilly Leaves, page 18. Petals points will be tacked down <u>after</u> the holly leaves are applied.

To make the poinsettia centers, use the 1/4"-wide ribbon and follow the instructions for Flower Centers, page 19.

Small Poinsettias

For a poinsettia design with multiple flowers, use the directions above for the large flowers. To make smaller poinsettias, use an additional 3/4 yard of 3/4"-wide ribbon for each flower. Cut the ribbon into five 5" to 6" long pieces. Stitch and assemble like the large poinsettia, but with one layer of petals. Add a ribbon center knotting an additional 1/2 yard of 1/4"-wide ribbon.

Holly

To make the holly leaves, trace the three holly patterns onto the matte side of the fusible stabilizer. Rough cut the holly patterns and fuse them to the Ultrasuede wrong side, with the leaf length on the crosswise grain. Cut out each leaf and remove the pattern; reuse the pattern for additional leaves. (Design shown at the chapter beginning has 14 leaves.)

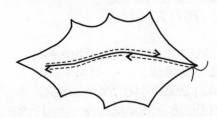

Pin a leaf over each end of the stem and arrange the remaining leaves along the cord. Straight stitch (3mm), leaves with the machine embroidery thread, starting at the stem and continuing along the vein lines.

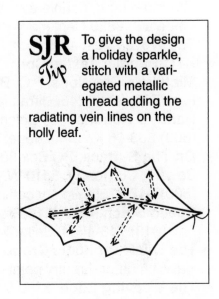

SJR Tip — To give the design a holiday sparkle, stitch with a variegated metallic thread adding the radiating vein lines on the holly leaf.

Bartack the poinsettia petal points with invisible thread in the machine needle. The petal sides may also need to be tacked in some places as the grosgrain ribbon is uncrushable and the tack holds it in position.

Sew on the button "berries" along the holly stem.

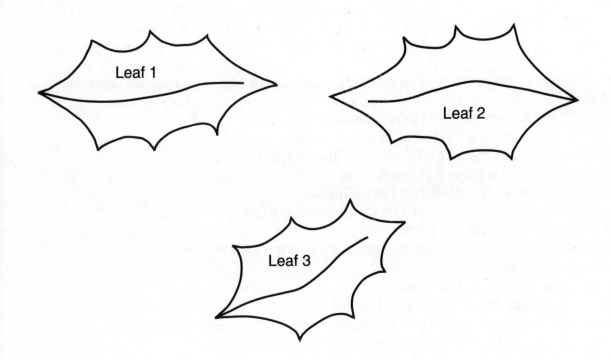

Leaf 1

Leaf 2

Leaf 3

Sources

Support your local retailer. If you cannot find the products listed in the book refer to these companies.

- **Clotilde Inc.**, B3000, Louisiana, MO 63353-3000, Phone (800) 772-2891.
  Wonder Tape, double-eye, yarn cards, stabilizers.
- **Ghee's®,** 2620 Centenary Blvd., #2-250, Shreveport, LA 71104, Phone (318) 226-1701.
  The Woven Vest #995
- **HTC-Handler Textile Corp.**, See your nearest retailer for stabilizers and fleece.
- **Michiko's Creations**, P.O. Box 4313, Napa, CA 94558, Phone (707) 224-8546,
  Fax (707) 224-2246. Ultrasuede.
- **Nancy's Notions,** 333 Beichl Ave., PO Box 683, Beaver Dam, WI 53916-0683, Phone
  (800) 833-0690. Ultrasuede, stabilizers, yarn cards, double-eye needles.
- **On The Surface**, PO Box 8026, Wilmette, IL 60091, Phone (847) 256-7446. Yarn cards.
- **Sew/Fit Company**, 5310 W. 66th St., Unit A, Bedford Park, IL 60638, Phone
  (800) 547-1739. Rotary cutting mats.
- **Speed Stitch, Inc.**; 3113 Broadpoint Dr., Harbor Heights, FL 33983, Phone (800) 874-4115,
  Fax (813) 743-4634. Sulky® of America. Stabilizers, decorative threads.
- **The Olfa® Products Group**, 2578 W. Park Dr., Murfreesboro, TN 37129. Pinking cutter,
  wave blade and rotary point cutter.
- **The Weaving Edge**, 3350 British Woods, Roanoke, VA 24019, Phone (540) 992-3497.
  Decorative yarns.
- **Total Embellishment Newsletter**, 142 Braewick Rd., Salt Lake City, UT 84103, Fax
  (801) 533-0481. Newsletter.
- **UltraMouse LTD.**, 3433 Bennington Ct., Bloomfield Hills, MI 48301, Phone (800) 225-1887.
  Ultrasuede.

Trademarks and Brand Names

Every effort has been made to properly credit the trademarks and brand names listed in this publication.

- APPLIQ-Ease™ is a trademark of HTC-Handler Textile Corp.
- Easy Stitch™ is a trademark of HTC-Handler Textile Corp.
- Fusible Fleece™ is a trademark of HTC-Handler Textile Corp.
- Husqvarna Viking™ is a trademark of Husqvarna
- Ribbon Floss™ is a trademark of Rhode Island Textiles
- Rotary Point Cutter is a brand name of The Olfa® Products Group
- Sliver™ is a trademark of Sulky® of America
- Soft & Flexible Velcro® is a registered trademark of Velcro USA Inc.
- Solvy™ is a trademark of Sulky® of America
- Stiffy™ is a trademark of Sulky® of America
- Totally Stable™ is a trademark of Sulky® of America
- Ultrasuede® and Ultrasuede Light® are registered trademarks of Springs Industries
- Wave/Pinking Cutter is a brand name of The Olfa® Products Group
- Wonder Tape is a brand name of W. H. Collins Inc.